THE EVERYDAY GUIDE TO OPENING AND OPERATING A CHILD CARE CENTER

by

Daniel F. Kingsbury
Sally Kweskin Vogler
Christine Benero

VADE MECUM PRESS
1500 West Alameda
Denver, CO 80223

Library of Congress Cataloging-in-Publication Data
Kingsbury, Daniel F. 1952-
The everyday guide to opening and operating a child care center.

Includes bibliographical references.
1. Day care centers – United States. I. Vogler, Sally Kweskin, 1955- . II. Benero, Christine, 1960- . III. Title.
HV854.K54 1990 362.7'12'068 89-22754

ISBN 0-945847-03-3

Printed and bound in the United States of America

Dedication

To the young children of the world, in whom we entrust our future—for they not only need, but more importantly deserve, the very best child care we can provide.

Acknowledgments

Special thanks to Frank Splitt, without whom this book would not have been written.

Thanks also to: Kam Moriarty, Diane Reeves, LaNola Clark, Elizabeth Rada Carver, Debby Jump, Sue Okerson, Beth Pfalmer, Ralph Moore, Ann Chandler, Richard Sheehan, the entire staff and Board of Directors of the Work and Family Consortium and the child care advocates for children who have contributed in one way or another to the completion of this book.

Preface

1) Child Care: Chi(ə)ld Ke(ɐ)r—Ka(ə)r\ n,adj 1. the care or supervision of another's child, especially at a day care center. 2. of or pertaining to or providing child care.
Random House Unabridged Dictionary: 1989

2) "An environment conducive to promoting a sense of well being, self-worth, and achievement within a child, as well as supporting, inspiring, and educating the child's parents."
Kam: Child care provider for 10 years.

3) "A safe place to leave my children while I work."
Shelley: Mother of Jenny, 2 1/2 years, and Steven, 1 year.

4) " A place to play."
Abby: Age 5.

Child care, *the* hot issue of our times, actually has roots that can be traced back to the days of the American colonies. History books document that in the early 1800's, Robert Owen's child care facility in New Harmony, Indiana, had over 100 children enrolled.

In the mid-1800's, the Civil War effort precipitated a move toward the institutionalization of child care. In cities and towns across the country, day nurseries were springing up for children of working women to meet communities' changing needs.

World War II dramatically changed the way America viewed child care. With the onset of the war, severe labor shortages forced the War Manpower Commission to effectively and expediently recruit women into the labor force. From 1940 to 1945 the number of working women soared to over 20 million, peaking in 1945 when women constituted 38% of the work force.

As women began working outside the home, child care became a major issue for both the public and private sectors. Manufacturers realized that by providing child care they could employ more women, lower costs, and increase productivity. Originally intended to provide funds for public works and community facilities, The Lanham Act, passed by Congress in 1941, was interpreted to provide federal funds for child care in "war impacted" communities.

Almost fifty years later, child care advocates, parents, and employers are talking more passionately than ever of the demographics of the workforce, the need for quality care, and its impact on the economic development of this country. The U.S. Department of Labor's report, "WORKFORCE 2000," states, "By the end of the decade, the changes underway will produce an America that is in some ways unrecognizable from the one that existed only a few years ago."

Families and Child Care

In 1986, more than 40,000 child care centers were in operation across the United States with a capacity exceeding 2.1 million children. It is estimated there were 25 million children aged 13 and under at this time. By the year 2000, it is estimated 82% of all women in the United States between the ages of 25 and 34 will be in the workforce.

In response to the following facts, 32 states passed approximately 125 pieces of legislation related to child care and early childhood education. Corporate sector involvement is also on the rise.

FACT: Mothers of infants are the fastest growing segment of the labor force today. In 1988, for the first time in our country's history, 52% of new mothers with children under one year entered or re-entered the work force — a 108% increase since 1970.

FACT: Sixty percent of mothers whose youngest child is between the ages of two and three work outside the home; 68% of mothers with children under 18 are in the labor force—up from 49% in 1976.

FACT: In the mid 1980s less than five percent of American households fit the model of the "traditional" family where the father works outside the home and the mother stays home to care for the children.

FACT: Today, one in five children live in a single parent household, with 64% of single mothers in the workforce.

FACT: For the first time in several decades, the number of young children is increasing; from 19.6 million in 1980, to 21.2 million in 1988.

So, what does the future hold? While we can't quite peer into a crystal ball, the message is clear—as the demand for child care grows, so will the gap between available care options and the number of youngsters needing care. While child care may be "a place to play," it is also a vital community service which allows parents to work and has become a cornerstone for this country's future economic development.

Table of Contents

Introduction

In this changing world, we are discovering that the two-worker family is the rule rather than the exception. As a result, children are now being cared for by people other than their parents. It is projected that by 1990 one out of every two children under five years of age will have a mother in the labor force. These trends are expected to continue.

Child care is very much a responsibility shared by both parents. The number of single-father head of households has greatly increased. Traditional support systems have been unable to keep up with the rate and scope of changes in the family. A great need has been created for child care that provides a safe, healthy, and stimulating social and educational environment.

In the *The Everyday Guide to Opening and Operating a Child Care Center* we provide the keys for successfully launching and running a child care center. Whether you're an early childhood professional or an entrepreneur seeking a new business venture, the answers to virtually every question you may have are contained in these pages.

We guide you through the maze of rules and regulations surrounding this industry, provide suggestions for raising capital, working with employers, choosing a building, and setting up a classroom. You are also given guidelines for hiring staff, developing curriculum, working with parents and establishing center policies. Actual forms and checklists are included to make your job easier.

America's child care concerns are being addressed across the country through creative partnerships, entrepreneurial efforts, and well planned "dreams." *The Everyday Guide to Opening and Operating a Child Care Center* can help you discover how you can become a part of the ever-growing early childhood care and education field.

1

The Dream

"After approaching a potential investor who happened to be the father of one of my partners, with our business plan to open a child care center, he commented: 'What you have here is a dream and a scheme. I'm not sure it'll work—but it sounds like a good dream and a good scheme.' He was willing to give us some financial backing and we were off."

Child Care Center Owner

Anyone planning to start or run a child care center must have a dream. Behind all the work and all the effort—and it will be different for different people—is a dream. It is the most important part of your plan.

What is the dream? It is the idea, the concept, the light that goes on in someone's head: "I'm going to open a child care center," "I'm going to start a preschool." Whatever it may be, however extensive, whatever form the plan may eventually take, it is the dream that will give you the energy and the encouragement you will need to pull it off.

Where does the dream come from? For some, it starts in childhood. They have a concept in their head that this is what they want to do, this is what they want to be. They seek involvement with young children. Oftentimes, a caregiver, parent, or relative who works with children becomes a role model to be emulated.

More often, the dream begins to emerge further down the road. It may arrive when they're in high school or in college, emerging from a positive experience they've had or class studies they are taking that lead them into a career in child care. Oftentimes, someone may be well established in another vocation, then decide they want to do something that will more personally embody their thoughts and beliefs. For others, it may be the sensing of a need and deciding to do something about it.

Types of Programs

"I went to a child care program in the Boston suburbs that has been in existence for at least 30 years. It was a parochial program that was operated by a small group of very caring nuns.

I remember that program as being fun and games! As an adult, looking back to that program, I think what a good way to introduce the idea of group care to a young child, to learn about sharing, listening to others, and figuring out how to stand up for myself. I guess one of the most important concepts for me was learning that there was "life without mommy" and that the idea of going to school might just be more fun than I thought."

Child Care Center Owner

There are a number of child care programs and services offered to parents within a community. Each option has advantages and disadvantages for you as an operator and for families seeking services.

Center-Based Programs

Child care centers are usually designed to meet the needs of working parents by operating all day, year around. Several types of centers exist, including large, small, infant nurseries, toddler nurseries, and day camps. The type of center is determined by the age of the children attending the program, purpose of the program, size of the group, and the teacher/child ratio.

Many centers serve children ages 2 1/2 to 5 years, although some are designed just for infants and toddlers. Others combine infants, toddlers, preschoolers, and in some situations, school-aged children.

Parent Cooperatives

A parent co-op is a program run and staffed by parents of the children who are enrolled. Many parent co-ops start simply as friendly neighborhood partnerships where two or more parents get together and come up with a child care plan. On Tuesday, for instance, parent

A will care for the children; on Wednesday, parent B; and on the following Thursday, parent C will do the honors. In this manner, parents are free of caregiving responsibilities for two out of the three days.

Many well established parent co-ops with large enrollments have hired staff and administrators. Parents may only supplement paid staff in a volunteer, cooperative effort.

Preschool Programs

Preschool programs come in many shapes and sizes and have nearly as many schedules and routines. A traditional preschool program typically involves two and a half to three hour sessions, three to five days per week for children aged 2 1/2 to 5 years. Parents may choose preschool programs to offer their children an opportunity to socialize with other youngsters and to be educationally stimulated. Preschools are designed to provide stimulating and challenging experiences for a short period of time. They are not generally used by parents who need full-day care.

Preschool programs are often located in community buildings such as schools, churches or community centers. You often find preschool programs within other types of child care programs. Child care centers may offer a part-time preschool program. The curriculum may not differ in content from the full-time program, but is designed, time wise, especially for those families seeking this type of service. In addition, many areas have child development centers or "lab schools" at local colleges where students of early childhood are trained.

In addition to preschools, centers, and parent co-ops, there are a myriad of other child care options including family child care homes, in-home providers, head-start programs, before and after school programs, and summer camps. The local Resource and Referral Agency in your community will have a complete listing of the types of care available.

Making the Dream Come True: Developing Your Business Plan

Once you have decided you want to open a child care center, your next step is to define what it is you intend to do. Develop a clear-cut plan of what the dream truly looks like. You have a dream—you know where you want to go. This step involves figuring out how to get there. It will take careful consideration on your part to decide exactly what type of service or services you want to offer and to realistically evaluate your level of commitment, plus your limitations and capabilities.

This process of taking the idea from a dream stage to a plan of action can be complicated. Done with forethought and imagination, however, it is the road map to your final destination. It will guide you step-by-step on your trip. It is what turns your dream into reality.

Understand What You're Getting Into

Prepare to answer the hard questions a business plan requires of you. As the initial phase of your plan, find out what opening and operating a child care center really means. Become well informed on the subject matter you have chosen. Open your eyes and ears to everything around you that deals with child care. Find out all you can about child care in your community, and at state and national levels. Child care is taking on a new face as we enter the 1990s, and it is important to be aware of the changes and factors that are involved in providing good care for America's families.

- Request a copy of the rules and regulations governing the provision of child care in the state where you plan to operate your center. It is critically important to understand what will be required of you regarding buildings, staff and government agencies.

- Meet other professionals in the field. Find out about local support networks and advocacy groups that can put you in touch with community issues and common problems.

- If you plan to direct your center, be sure to find out what course work or experience is required for you to qualify for that position.

- Prepare yourself for the future. Enroll in pertinent classes or workshops in the field that may be applied toward required certifications.

- Start gathering printed information. There are several key child care magazines. Among others are the *Child Care Information Exchange, Child Care Review, Young Children,* a publication of the National Association for the Education of Young Children, and *Pre-K Today* by Scholastic. Many popular periodicals published in this country today also deal with child care. There are articles in virtually every magazine from *Time* to *Psychology*

Today, and in more localized media such as newspapers and area parent publications. There are also a number of books about child care—more than 5,000 were published in the 1980s. It is virtually impossible for one person to purchase all of these books, let alone read them. Select those that are most appealing to you. Your local libraries will also have an abundance of information on the subject.

- Observe existing child care programs. Most centers welcome information seekers. Many programs have established visiting policies and "open house" schedules so someone seeking information about child care can ask questions and observe in the classroom. In many cases, centers have set up classroom opportunities where you can volunteer and get firsthand experience in dealing with young children.

Observing child care programs is particularly important if you have had limited experience or educational background in early childhood education. For prospective owners or directors that have experience and training in the field, it is no less important to observe other program models. Pay particular attention to the classroom environment, room arrangement, overall scheduling and planning for a child's day, staffing schedules, hiring policies, playground use and supervision, parent interaction, and the implementation of the early childhood program.

Seek out all sources of information. Read, observe, network, question. In the process, you will come across theories, practices, and viewpoints with which you wholeheartedly agree—and those with which you disagree vehemently. When you understand the issues affecting the child care industry, you will enter the field with your eyes wide open. You will have an understanding of what child care really means and have direction on how best to provide it.

When You're Ready: Think It Through

The business plan should include the following: what you want to accomplish, what type of service you want to offer and who your clientele will be. You'll also want to address location, marketing strategies, and a plan for securing financial resources. If you can answer these issues concisely and thoroughly, you are on your way to starting a successful operation.

1. WHAT DO YOU WANT TO ACCOMPLISH?
   Only you know what your ultimate goals are. Do you want to run your own business? To positively impact a new generation? To offer the "model" child care center? Is profit your main motivation? Do you want to immerse yourself in your work or maintain a distance from your business? Do you want to start a chain of centers?

2. WHAT TYPE OF SERVICE DO YOU WANT TO OFFER?
   In determining what kind of service you want to offer, you will also define how you will serve families. It is important to understand that to have a successful child care program you must determine families' needs and meet them. In this way, you set the parameters for who will seek you out and use the services for which you have so carefully planned.
   The service you offer should be in demand in the community. What does your area need? Is it a preschool program, parent co-op, or a full-day/full-week child care center? What location would be best? What kind of facility will you need? What space requirements will you have? Will you build, buy, or lease?

3. WHO WILL YOUR CLIENTELE BE?
   In order to be successful in your endeavor, you must first determine whether or not there are families who will use your services. Since both children and parents are your clients, consider their perceptions and needs in designing your program.   How many children will you serve and what age groups?

4. HOW WILL YOU MARKET YOUR PROGRAM?
   Unless people know your program is available, they won't use it. How do you plan to alert the community to your child care center? What will draw people to your program as opposed to another?

5. HOW WILL YOU SECURE FINANCIAL BACKING?
Typically, you must make a large initial investment to open a child care center. To make your investment worthwhile you must consider organizational structure, such as profit versus nonprofit status. Will you attempt to do this yourself, or involve partners? Do you have sufficient capital to finance the operation? If you'll need loans, what can you offer as collateral?

6. IS YOUR BUSINESS PLAN COMPATIBLE WITH YOUR EDUCATIONAL PHILOSOPHY?
What will your early childhood program be like? How many children do you want in each room? How many teachers? What will your fees be? Are they competitive? After insurance, rent, utilities, and other expenses, can you project a profit? Will you break even? If you plan to build a facility, will it be worth your investment over the long run?
With a dream you believe in, and a carefully designed business plan, success is indeed within your grasp!

2

Developing Your Early Childhood Program

The success of your business will be based in large part on the quality of your early childhood program—, what children experience during the time they are in your care. As parents become more informed consumers and begin to understand the importance of their children's early education, they will select child care on the basis of its program—as well the appeal of the facilities, fees, and hours. As someone who is responsible for the early childhood care and education of young children, you cannot afford to offer anything less than an excellent program.

What Is a Quality Early Childhood Care and Education Program?

Professional child care varies in quality. This somewhat elusive concept is determined by many things, including the personal characteristics of the child care staff, their level of training, the physical environment of the center, and the opportunity for parent involvement. As a child care center operator, you should be familiar with what researchers and child care experts have identified as indicators of quality child care. Your program should be firmly based on knowledge of what constitutes healthy environments for young children. Following are some "indicators" of quality child care:

SPECIALIZED TRAINING OF THE STAFF

Provider training is one of the most critical factors affecting the quality of child care. Teachers who have received child-related education have been shown to provide a more stimulating, enriched environment for children. They are more responsive and comforting, and spend more time talking and socializing directly with children.

TEACHER-CHILD INTERACTION

Children flourish in humane environments where they are treated with positive regard and respect. Caregivers should be affectionate, energetic, and warm with children. Both boys and girls—plus children of all races, religious or ethnic backgrounds—should have the same opportunities to participate in program activities and events. Discipline should be viewed as an opportunity for children to learn.

GROUP SIZE

The number of children enrolled in a classroom has a significant influence on both the teachers and children. Children in smaller groups are more cooperative and more task-oriented. They are more elaborate in their play, and are more talkative and interactive with their peers.

STAFF TO CHILD RATIO

The number of staff caring for children compared with the number of children in attendance is often referred to as the "staff to child ratio." This ratio seems to be important, particularly for infants and toddlers. A caregiver responsible for a high number of children is unable to be as responsive as one who cares for fewer young ones.

PROGRAM/CURRICULUM

There are a variety of approaches to education for young children. While researchers have not identified one model as being better than another, it is important programs have a written educational philosophy and established goals for children. Educational programs should by nature, be sensitive to the age group of children they serve, and the individual needs of each child in the group. This is often referred to as developmentally appropriate practice.

STAFF STABILITY

The length of time a staff member remains with a group of children affects the teacher-child relationship. The issue of consistency of care givers is important because the development of secure relationships with adults is important for the young child.

PARENT PARTICIPATION

Research shows children will be more likely to have a successful school experience if their parents are actively involved in their education. Child care programs should offer on-going opportunities for parent involvement (i.e., parent conferences, open visitation, parent newsletters, and volunteer activities).

SAFETY/HEALTH

It is essential all children be cared for in a safe and clean environment. Among other things, children should be supervised at all times, first aid supplies should be accessible, and an emergency plan and sick child policy should be established.

NUTRITION/FOOD SERVICE

The food children are served in a child care program should be well balanced and represent food from the four food groups. Children should be allowed to eat as their appetite dictates. They should not be forced to eat, nor punished or rewarded on the basis of eating. Eating should be a social experience, relaxed and conversational.

RESOURCES FOR CHILDREN

Programs should have enough equipment to be accessible to all children in attendance. Equipment should be in good repair, and be challenging and stimulating for the age group of children using it. The program should offer both opportunities for children to spend time with larger groups of youngsters and have some private time as well.

WHO IS RESPONSIBLE FOR THE PROGRAM?

Depending upon the size of your program, your desired level of involvement, and your knowledge of how young children grow and develop, a child care owner or director may be responsible for designing the early childhood program. If you have a limited background in early childhood education, you might consider hiring a program director to be responsible for the day-to-day design and management of curriculum and practices in the classroom. If you feel you are capable of doing this yourself but need additional information, there are a great many resources to assist you.

Developing a Philosophy of Early Childhood Education

An integral part of your business plan is to commit to writing your educational philosophy. This is not only a marketing tool, but is often a standard licensing requirement. It will be the foundation on which your activity plans or curriculum is built. This theoretical foundation directly impacts the way teachers function in the classroom, the way the classroom is set up, the materials available to children, the goals and objectives of your program, the daily schedule, your curriculum, and the way you work with parents. Consider the following questions and address each in your statement of philosophy:

Philosophy Statement

- How do you think young children learn?
- What would be your purpose or goal of education for the young child?
- What is the teacher's role in early childhood education?
- What should a schedule and daily routine look like?
- How do we allow for individual consideration of children? Consideration of the group?
- What is the parent's role in early childhood education?
- How is discipline handled with children? What is the goal of discipline?
- What is the importance of competition? Does it have a place in the early childhood classroom?
- What is child care? What kind of experience should children have while they are in attendance? What are your long-term goals for youngsters who attend your program?

SAMPLE: Philosophy Statement

Example I.
      "It is impossible to portray in words the functioning of a system in which every part is related to every other in such a

way that each has a causal influence on the others." Conrad Lorenz

"We believe that children have the right to a nurturing, safe environment where they can feel comfortable and secure. We believe that children have a right to develop to their maximum abilities and that teachers have the responsibility to provide opportunities for this development to occur.

"We recognize that each child is an individual and that each child must be allowed to develop at his or her own pace. We accept and respect differences between children including developmental and physical differences and differences in racial and ethnic heritages. Every child regardless of sex, race, religion or ethnic origin must have the same opportunities and advantages as every other child.

"We believe each child has the right to develop a positive self image—to feel good about who they are. We fervently hope that in treating each child with love and respect that they in turn will learn to treat others with that same love and respect.

"We believe that children learn best through active participation with their environment and that the teacher's job is to provide a variety of opportunities and experiences to promote growth in all areas. We strive to thoughtfully plan activities that meet the developmental needs of differing children and which follow sound early childhood developmental principles."

Philosophy statement courtesy of the Auraria Child Care Center, Denver, Colorado.

Example II.

"The goal of the center is to support each child's development to his/her potential in all areas of growth and learning.

"The staff promotes a child's good feelings about himself/herself through loving caregiving. We know that feelings of self-worth, meaningful peer and adult relationships, feelings of competence in cognitive skills and physical well-being are most important to the young child. Each child is valued for his/her uniqueness and individuality.

"Our respect for children is visible through the day in the way we talk with children, give choices in play, set up the environment, offer challenging and varied experiences which encourage creativity, and follow the interest of children in our center.

"We know that to reach our goal we must work cooperatively with parents sharing in our mutual interest in the child."

Philosophy statement courtesy of the Jeanne C. Simon Child Care Center, a member of the Visiting Nurse Foundation Family, Burlington, Vermont.

SAMPLE: Educational Goals

Example I.

EDUCATIONAL GOALS FOR THE YOUNG CHILD

• We want children to learn to work and play independently; to have the opportunity to develop positive relationships with their peers and adults. To help this happen staff must be emotionally accessible, consistent, and model healthy interactions with other staff members and children.

• We want children to develop a positive sense of self esteem—a belief that they are able to accomplish whatever they set out to do; that they are good and valuable people that like other people as well as themselves. To help this happen staff should use every opportunity to help children develop a realistic self concept through the use of reflection and descriptive praise.

• We want children to learn to live compatibly with other people and understand that everyone's needs and beliefs should be respected. To help this happen staff must teach children the art of problem-solving, consensus building, and positive conflict resolution.

• We want children to be culturally aware. We want them to gain an understanding that although people of the world look different, use different languages, and have a wide variety of values and customs, that these differences don't make them any more or less valuable. To help this happen concepts of cultural diversity must be incorporated into the daily curriculum.

• We want children to develop a love of learning, to be able to ask questions, do research, and use available resources effectively. To help this happen staff must create a safe environment, rich with opportunity to explore and construct and extend learning.

• We want children to become familiar with their creative talents—drama, the arts, dance, music—to feel that this creative side has value and brings a sense of beauty into their life. To help this happen staff must offer children the opportunity to explore the arts/creative outlets.

- We want children to learn that work is not always easy but is often hard; to persevere, to follow things through to their end, to feel determined to find answers. To help this happen staff must help children work through frustration, extend learning experiences, and support them individually in their work.

- We want children to believe that they must give back to the world; that they share the world with many people, and must take an active role in making sure it is well cared for. To help this happen staff must introduce concepts of environment in a developmentally appropriate manner, and model and encourage cooperation and a sense of social responsibility.

- We want children to take pride in themselves physically, to take care of their bodies, to establish a pattern of healthy physical routines. We help this to happen by talking and reading about the human body, providing opportunity to develop and test physical skills, and by modeling healthy practices (i.e., toothbrushing, nutritionally sound meals, exercise, hand washing.)

- We want children to feel comfortable with emotion, to be capable of managing feelings of anger, sorrow, fear, joy in a healthy manner. To help this happen staff must accept emotion, guide children in rechanneling unproductive reactions, and help children to verbalize their feelings.

- We want children to feel comfortable and effective with using language as a means of communication in all of its forms: poetry, art, song, puppetry, written and spoken. To help this happen staff must create a language rich environment where children's efforts in writing, speaking, singing, painting are valued.

  — developed by S. Kweskin, 1986

Example II.

The following set of curriculum goals is meant as an overview of the XYZ Center program. Although the goal statements are divided into different areas of growth and development, each area is interactive and interrelated to the other areas.

Yourself and Others

1. To provide opportunities for children to grow as individuals and experience feelings of self-worth.

2. To promote a healthy self concept by encouraging the development of trust and security.

3. To encourage the development of independence and self help skills.

4. To encourage the development of social skills such as cooperation and respect for others.

5. To encourage the interaction of children with other children and adults and small and large group settings.

Language

1. To encourage children to develop the verbal skills necessary to communicate feelings, thoughts, and needs.

2. To expose children to an accepting environment rich in language opportunities including the development of listening skills, written and oral communication skills.

Physical Growth

1. To provide a safe, secure environment in which children can explore the space around them and learn to use their bodies with control.

2. To develop an awareness in children of the importance of taking care of one's body, by exposure to sound nutritional practices and physical fitness goals.

3. To provide the children with a variety of opportunities to practice fine and gross motor skills according to each child's developmental needs and abilities.

Active Learning

1. To offer children a variety of activities that aid in their intellectual and cognitive growth according to developmental principles.

2. To allow children to actively explore the attributes and functions of materials with all their senses.

3. To encourage the discovery of relations through direct experience.

4. To provide opportunities for predicting problems and devising ways of solving them.

5. To encourage the development of creativity and imagination.

Goals courtesy of Shirley Stafford, Susan Turner, Tina Roybal, Diane Klein, and Crystal Abeyta of the Auraria Child Care Center.

What's the Best Way for Children to Learn?: Play Is the Way

When Caroline comes to school in the morning, she is ready to see her friends and play. When Sage arrives, he tells his dad "See you later, I'm going to play with my friends!" or "I'm going to play in the art area." Their parents somewhat resignedly tell others that all their child does at school is play.

What most people do not understand is that the primary occupation of most young children is play. Play is the mechanism through which children learn and form the basis for all future learning; it is children's way of making sense of the world and resolving issues in their lives. It is early childhood care and education at its best.

Life is a carnival to young children: a place for doing, for discovering and trying things out. Young children learn by processing the "sensory information" they acquire by seeing, hearing, touching, tasting, and smelling. Learning is accomplished when children have the opportunity to actively explore their world at their own pace. It occurs when they can test what it is they have discovered and repeat the same process over and over again until they make sense of what they have found.

Unlike older children, preschoolers, toddlers, and infants are unable to efficiently and effectively translate words into meaningful solutions to the questions they have about the world.

Instead, they must act on the object or environment in a "hands-on" way, and discover answers, properties, relationships, skills, and concepts for themselves.

As an egocentric being (someone who is only able to see the world from his or her own perspective), the young child learns best when he or she experiences things that are meaningful to him or her at that given time. In addition, youngsters do not separate learning experiences according to the teacher's planned activity. One cannot separate the dimensions in which the child experiences learning. The child learns totally; the whole of the child is affected. Activities may result in social, emotional, intellectual, creative, or physical growth.

Joanie and Mike are playing in the block center. They are working together to build a town with houses, lakes, roads, and buildings, As they build, Joanie notices that some blocks cannot support the weight or length of other blocks, and that when they are not supported, they fall to the ground. She finds when she puts several blocks on top of each other, her building grows taller. Mike finds he needs four blocks of the same size to make square houses and buildings. For the round pond, he must use curved blocks.

As a result of this play-based activity, Mike and Joanie are learning concepts of weight, size, balance, construction, gravity, and symmetry. They are learning to work cooperatively on a project, to create something from their imagination, and to improve their fine motor skills by moving and balancing the blocks.

Planning Your Curriculum

While older children may be more capable of translating symbols such as words and numbers into learning, to the young child they are merely undigested pieces of information. While drill and memorization exercises may be appropriate for older children, direct instruction (teacher lecturing to a group) fails to recognize how young children learn and grow.

Curriculum should be carefully developed by staff and administrators that have classroom experience, knowledge of child development theory, and current research findings. When planning a curriculum for use in the classroom, you should consider:

- Human beings develop according to a predictable and orderly pattern. Aspects of development vary, however, from individual to individual. Thus, we can expect and anticipate certain kinds of behaviors, and determine predictable actions and skill levels across the age spans.

  Planning must take into account the *developmental levels* of the group of children for which it is designed. Plans will differ dramatically for infants, toddlers, and preschoolers, just as they will differ for individual children within a given classroom.

- Young children are egocentric by nature. They are unable to consider or comprehend another person's point of view or frame of reference. As a result, teachers must capitalize and take advantage of children's interests so that play becomes learning to the child.

  Planning must be flexible to accommodate for the differing interests of children. Curriculum plans should not force children to learn only things the teacher finds of interest.

- There are particularly sensitive periods at which optimum learning of some kind can occur for a child if the opportunity to learn is present.

  Curriculum plans must be broad-based and provide plenty of

opportunity for children to choose what it is they will do. Based on teachers' observations of children in action in the classroom, they can support and facilitate the needs of individual children with respect to their timetables and educational growth.

- Activities should be open-ended. They need to focus on the "process" rather than the product. To stimulate and encourage creativity, children must be allowed to design and create products that are uniquely theirs, not modeled after an adult's work.

Sample: Daily Planning Sheet

Date:_____ Area of Emphasis_____

<u>Group and Individual Goals and Objectives:</u>

WORK/PLAY ACTIVITIES	PROCEDURE	QUESTIONS/ EXTENSIONS	MATERIALS	PREPARATION

CIRCLE TIME ACTIVITIES:

SMALL GROUP ACTIVITIES:

The Process of Planning

Because kids approach learning differently, and are interested in different things, planning must have the flexibility to meet individual children's needs. By observing youngsters in the classroom, teachers can identify what subjects are of interest to them. Specific activities or materials designed to encourage and extend learning for the individual and for the group are then incorporated into planning. For the teacher in a *developmentally based* program (one which tailors the program to meet the developmental needs of the young child), planning is flexible and can be based almost entirely on the interest of children, rather than a predetermined set of activities and discussion topics.

Children need a teacher who is responsive and who supports their learning style, not someone who directs and instructs based on his or her own interest and needs. Child-oriented activities are designed to establish goals and objectives for children rather than to just keep them busy. Goals and objectives differ from child to child.

Elena has been talking for several days about her collection of rings. She has asked if she can bring them in and show them to other children. After hearing this, several other children talk about collections they have at home.

Teachers see this as an opportunity to broaden and expand children's interest and pride in their personal collections. They incorporate into tomorrow's plans a *show and tell* time for children to share their treasures. At group time, the children make up a story about them. They plan to include some activities that focus on classification and sorting skills, locate some children's books on collections, plan a field trip to the local museum to look at the fossil collection, take a nature walk to collect similar types of objects (leaves and rocks for instance) that children can place in old egg cartons. They bring in some gold stars, tinfoil and old beads so Elena can make herself another ring for her collection.

Debby and Tom are early childhood teachers who share responsibility for a group of 20 three-year-olds. They are enthusiastic and excited about including lots of fun activities in their planning. They spend planning time determining what they will cover in the next month. Since Tom knows a lot about dinosaurs, they decide children in their classroom will learn about dinosaurs for the next two weeks. Their curriculum or planning sheet is filled with a myriad of activities that relate to dinosaurs.

The next week in circle time, Tom wants the children to talk about why dinosaurs died. Several members of the group want to talk about their grandparents and why they died. Tom asks them to stop talking about that and to concentrate on dinosaurs. As they continue, some of the children become restless in the group and do not want to participate in the discussion. Instead of taking this chance to discuss death and grieving, Tom forces the group to concentrate on a subject that interests *him*. In the process, he stifles a rare learning opportunity.

The importance of "planning time" cannot be overstated. Your educational program is the heart of your business. In order to support teachers in providing high quality child care programs, you must be sure classrooms are staffed with adequate numbers of teachers and aides to allow for the development of curriculum and daily plans. Many centers designate planning time for supervising teachers during the work day.

Although there are a variety of ways teachers design their learning experiences, the way the planning is done is less important than the fact that some sort of actual planning takes place. Planning reflects the teacher's, director's, or owner's educational philosophy. While some teachers find it can only be done on a daily basis in order to speak to children's interests, others plan activities on a weekly or monthly basis. Most frequently, plans revolve around a theme or unit of study, such as seasons, and holidays, shapes, However planning is designed, it is important the curriculum is flexible and open to input from children.

Scheduling the Day

Most early childhood teachers and associate teachers arrange their day in such a way that it suits children's needs as well as their own. Because many child-care programs last up to 10 or 11 hours a day for full-time care, daily schedules include breakfast, lunch, snack times, nap, clean-up time, and time for hand washing and tooth brushing. For infants and toddlers, time will be included for diaper changing and toilet training. Days should be organized so children have the opportunity to relax and have quiet time as well as plenty of chances to be active.

Work time is defined as those periods of the day when children are involved in activities (planned or unplanned) and using equipment.

This does not mean to imply that work time is a time when children must be quiet and concentrate on completing tasks. Play is the work of young children. While they are playing, they are working and learning.

WORK TIME is characterized by choice of materials, and child-initiated activity. Free play is discovery oriented, and children are encouraged to explore, imagine, invent, express feelings, display emotions and enjoy themselves.

CIRCLE TIMES or group times are typically part of the daily schedule; they can last up to 30 minutes for preschoolers or be as short as five minutes for toddlers. Group times are not appropriate for infants or young toddlers. During this time, the group focuses on some activity that has been planned by the teacher. Circle times may include singing, reading books, storytelling, sharing experiences, and puppet shows.

SMALL GROUP is included in many early childhood programs. Generally, it is a time where children are divided into small groups that work with a teacher on a given activity or subject.

MEALTIME should be a relaxed social experience. Teachers should eat with children. Mealtimes should last as long as is developmentally appropriate for the age group being served: 10 to 30 minutes for toddlers, 15 to 30 minutes for preschoolers. Time scheduled for meals should be flexible—some days children will want to spend a longer time at a table than other days. Children should be encouraged to serve themselves in a family manner. While kids should not be forced to eat, encouragement is sometimes appropriate.

REST TIME is an important event for young children in full-day care. Teachers can do several things to help settle children down and make resting a peaceful experience. Darkening the room, playing soft music, reading stories, and giving back rubs helps. Children should be allowed to bring a personal "cuddly" to school to snuggle with at nap time. Teachers must be sensitive to those children who no longer require naps and plan alternative activities of a quiet nature.

Sample Daily Schedules

TODDLER
ACTIVITY PLAN FOR WEEK OF _____

T h e m e   f o r   t h e   w e e k

Monday	Tuesday	Wednesday	Thursday	Friday
7:00-8:00	Children Arrive/ Open Classroom Time			
8:00-8:15	Clean-Up Time			
8:15-8:30	Group Time			
8:30-8:45	Wash-Up/Have Breakfast or Snack			
8:45-9:15	Clean-Up/Diapers/Toilet/Open Classroom Time			
9:15-11:00	Open Classroom to Include Pre-Planned Activities Development Within Theme/Self- Initiated Activities/Choice of Materials (Diapers and Toilet As Needed)			
11:00-11:30	Clean-Up/Wash-Up For Lunch			
11:30-12:00	Lunch (Time May be Expanded-Do Not Rush)			
12:00-12:30	Clean-Up/Diapers/Toilet/Books on Individual Mats, or in Cribs			
12:30-2:00	Rest Time			
2:00-3:00	Wake-Up/Diapers/Toilet Quiet Pre-Planned Activities and Books (Good One-On-One Time)			
3:00-3:30	Snack Time			
3:30-5:00	Open Classroom To Include Pre-Planned Activities Development Within Theme/Self-Initiated Activities/Choice of Materials (Diapers And Toilet As Needed)			

Developed by Kam Moriarty, Work and Family Consortium, 1989
PRESCHOOL
DAILY SCHEDULE

7:00   ARRIVAL AND FREE PLAY
8:10   WASH UP/BREAKFAST
9:00   OUTDOOR PLAY
9:30   CIRCLE TIME
9:50   WORK TIME
11:00 SMALL GROUP ACTIVITY
11:30 QUIET TIME/PREPARATION FOR LUNCH
11:40 LUNCH/BRUSH TEETH
12:00 OUTDOOR TIME
12:50 PREPARATION FOR NAP
1:00   NAP TIME
3:00   NAP TIME CLEAN-UP
3:15   SNACK TIME
3:30   OUTDOOR TIME
4:15   AFTERNOON CIRCLE TIME
4:45   FREE EXPLORATION
5:35   CLEAN UP/STORIES

Schedule developed by Susan Turner, Susan Flaa, Trudy Kline-dienst and Vicki Lindquist; Osage Initiatives, Denver, CO.

KINDERGARTEN
DAILY SCHEDULE

8:00 - GOOD MORNING! PLANNING TIME	Breakfast is served until 8:50. As children arrive they go to the planning board or make a planning sheet for their morning work.
WORK TIME	A time of free exploration of materials and areas within the room. Teachers extend and suggest activities.
9:30 - CLEANUP TIME	Everybody helps.
10:00 - OUTDOOR TIME	A time for planned outdoor activity or free exploration of the yard.
10:30 - CIRCLE TIME	A time to be together for stories, songs, games and sharing.
11:00 - SMALL GROUP	Time to work with a small group usually on an activity.

11:30 - BIG ROOM TIME
12:00 - LUNCH
12:40 - OUTDOOR PLAY
1:30 - PREPARATION FOR REST TIME
1:45 - REST
2:45 - REST TIME CLEAN UP
3:00 - SNACK
3:20 - OUTDOOR PLAY
4:00 - AFTERNOON CIRCLE   Stories, songs, games.
4:30 - PROJECT TIME   A planned activity and free explo-
                           ration time.
5:00 - CLEAN UP
5:30 - GOODBYE   Quiet stories and games

Schedule courtesy of Shirley Stafford and Cindi Friedman, Auraria Child Care Center, 1988

The Role of the Teacher In the Classroom

The relationship between the early childhood teacher and the children in his or her classroom is among the most critical determinants of a quality program. Teachers are not only role models for children, they dramatically influence the atmosphere of the classroom.

• Teachers should support and build positive relationships with parents by opening up the classroom to them, encouraging them to feel a part of the program, and talking with them about their children.

• Teachers should help children learn to problem solve and extend thinking skills by creating an environment that is rich in opportunity to explore. They encourage creative thinking by asking open-ended questions that have more than one answer: "What do you think is going on here?" "I wonder what would happen if we changed this?" "How do you feel about that?"

• Teachers use every opportunity to foster competence in children's intellectual, physical, emotional-social, and creative dimensions by creating a climate that welcomes and encourages exploration, questioning, and risk-taking. They are responsible for stocking the classroom with materials that encourage learning to occur.

Their job is to provide a variety of opportunities and experiences to promote growth in all areas.

- Teachers observe and listen to young children at play. They facilitate active learning by using what they see to identify and support children's interests. They help the young child to understand his or her feelings and work through important issues.

- Teachers nurture, respect, and attend to children. Early childhood classrooms should be a place where children can make mistakes, then learn and grow from that experience. It should be a place where staff recognizes the inherent gifts of each child and uses that knowledge to challenge and encourage that youngster to reach his or her potential.

- Teachers promote a language-rich environment by encouraging conversation, and exposing children to language in any form through song, stories, finger plays, poetry, and puppetry.

Evaluating Your Program

With national attention focused on the issue of quality child care, the evaluation of quality programs has become more important than ever. As your child care program continues to evolve, you will want to evaluate your efforts on an ongoing basis. This can be done informally or through a more formal evaluation such as one designed by the National Association for the Education of Young Children . Their accreditation process is designed to:

- Help early childhood program personnel become involved in a process that will facilitate real and lasting improvements in the quality of the program serving young children; and to

- Evaluate the quality of the program for the purpose of accrediting those programs that substantially comply with the criteria for high quality programs.

NAEYC's accreditation program involves an in-depth self study, followed by an on-site visit to validate the center's self-study program description. Child care centers may voluntarily choose to participate in the accreditation process. If you decide not to participate in the entire process the *Accreditation Criteria and Procedures Manual* is well worth the investment as an evaluation guide.

Informally, there are several things you can observe at your center on a daily basis that will give you a sense of whether or not your program is functioning well.

Self evaluation: How healthy is your program?

Q: Are the children in your program happy to come to school?

Q: Is your enrollment stable? Are the families who use your service choosing to keep their children in your program over a period of time? Or are they leaving to find other programs?

Q: What is the average length of stay for your teachers? Is there high turnover among head and assisting teachers? Are they leaving because they are dissatisfied with the program?

Q: Does the center feel like a happy place? Are children actively engaged in play? Or is there a great deal of crying and fighting among children?

Q: Is your early childhood program designed to meet the needs of the group as well as individuals within the group? Is it solidly based on child development and is it child oriented?

Q: Is there plenty of developmentally appropriate equipment for children? Is it in good repair?

Q: Are children safe in your program? How many injuries did you have in the past month? Do you consider this too many? Could they have been prevented?

Q: Are your meals nutritious and appetizing? Are children eating the food? Is there always enough to go around?

Q: Do local teacher training programs use your center as a placement for their interns?

Q: Do you have an in-service training program for staff in place? Do you support your teachers in attending local conferences, workshops, or seminars on early childhood related matters?

Q: Are center policies clear cut and straightforward? When people have questions about administration, can you answer them? Are policies in place for administration, children, parents, and staff?

Q: Are parents actively involved in the program? Do they feel comfortable just dropping in? Are they volunteering in the classroom? Do they feel welcome when they walk in the center's doors?

3

Understanding Rules and Regulations

Three women were traveling together on a tour bus through the streets of London. The first woman exclaimed, "Oh, look! It's Wembley." The second woman said, "Oh, no! I think it's Thursday." And the third woman replied, "Oh, I'm thirsty too! Let's stop at the next pub!"

Everyday communication is sometimes elusive; communication with government agencies can seem impossible. Yet to become licensed to operate a child care center, you must comply with state rules and regulations governing them. Within each state a regulatory agency determines what type of child care programs will be required to comply and what the rules and regulations will be. The key to understanding rules and regulations is to develop a relationship with these agencies based on open communication.

At the close of this chapter is a list of each state's regulatory agencies governing child care facilities. Contact your state agency to get a copy of their minimum rules and regulations for child care facilities. Some charge a fee for sending you a copy. However, they are vital for a successful start in the child care business.

Highlights of Regulations
Across the Country

If the regulation of child care programs across this country is consistent in any aspect, it is only that regulations differ dramatically from state to state! If there is agreement on any level, it is that child care regulations are minimum standards below which no program may legally operate.

The most comprehensive comparison of child care regulations across the country is Gwen Morgan's, "The National State of Child Care Regulations—1986," which notes the following highlights and trends:

- Forty-one states have updated their requirements for child care centers in the last five years; 19 of them since 1985.

- Programs are considered developmental. Almost every state requires centers to provide a developmental program; only 3 have no wording to this effect for centers. The concept of custodial care is now obsolete in most geographic areas.

- There is a trend toward age- appropriate requirements. thirty-four (34) states have specific program requirements for infants/toddlers and 19 have specific program requirements for schoolage children. There is a trend toward age-appropriate requirements for each age group.

- Eighteen states regulate group size for preschool children. Twenty four states regulate it for infants and toddlers.

- There is a trend toward supporting parents' right to visit. Eighteen states give parents the legal right to visit at anytime. Thirty-eight states address parent visits in their center requirements.

- Twenty-six states require ongoing training for teachers and care givers.

- Six states have recently added that center directors must have courses in administration as well as child development.

- Eighteen states require training for all classroom teachers.

- Immunization for children in child care centers is almost universally required. Only three states—Arizona, Idaho, and Nebraska—do not have immunization requirements for children in care.

- Thirty-three states require, or are planning to require, criminal record checks in centers. Four other states check abuse records but not criminal records.

- Twenty-four states require liability insurance for child care centers.

Regulatory Agencies

In seven states, the health department is the licensing agency for child care centers. Five states have placed this responsibility with the office for children, and the remaining 38 states regulate child care through social services, human services, or welfare agencies.

Specific Rules and Regulations

PHYSICAL REQUIREMENTS: INDOOR SPACE

Rules vary from state to state for indoor space according to the age of the child served.

Infant:

Infant care often has a requirement for more indoor space than preschool care. This is because infants' apparatus, such as cribs and high chairs, take up more permanent space. In many states, if the activity area is separated from the sleeping area, then space requirements for the activity area are lowered. If the activity area and sleep area are combined, which is the case in many facilities, the space requirement is somewhat higher—typically 45 square feet per child.

Toddlers:

The space requirement for toddlers is typically 35 to 40 square feet per child. For toddler programs that have activity space separated from their sleep area, the space requirement may be lowered.

Preschool:

For preschool children aged three and up, the indoor space requirement is 30 to 35 square feet per child. This usually excludes areas not used for activity, such as bathrooms and hallways.

Other Physical Requirements

Your child care licensing department will also take a look at outdoor play space. Minimum requirements will be mandated. Generally speaking, a minimum of 1500 square feet is required for playgrounds. Some states require 75 square feet per child for at least one-third of the number of children for which your facility is licensed. This arrangement allows the playground to be used by one-third of the children at any given time. Alternating use of the playground is assumed.

Many states require a child care center to be located on the ground floor for accessibility to exits during an emergency. Some states do allow child care facilities serving older children to be on other than ground level.

AGE GROUPS

Many states require children of different ages be physically separated from one another in a child care setting. For example, an infant area may need to be separate from a toddler area, which needs to be separated from a preschool or pre-kindergarten area. Some states also require separate entryways for children of different age levels.

GROUP SIZE

Many states regulate group size. This is an important consideration when planning space for child care facilities. For example, if a state requires that group size for infants cannot exceed ten children, then it would be excessive to have a very large area for this limited number of children.

STAFF QUALIFICATIONS

Recent research indicates if there is one single factor most important in determining the quality of the staff, it is their child care related training and experience. Consequently, many regulatory agencies concern themselves with qualifications of staff and staff ratios, with particular focus on education and experience.

Qualifications for teaching staff may include course work dealing with early childhood education. In some cases, experience may be an accepted substitute for this course work. Directors might be required to have a two-year or four-year degree; they may also be required to have course work dealing with early childhood education, administration, nutrition, and counseling.

STAFF/CHILD RATIOS

The number of required staff to children differs from state to state. While some require a ratio of one adult to three children for infant care, others have a ratio of one adult to ten infants.

Other Regulatory Agencies

THE HEALTH DEPARTMENT

In most states, the health department has jurisdiction over those functions of a child care center dealing directly with food, food preparation, food handling, and sanitation. Large child care centers must often meet the same regulations as restaurants for food service practices.

The department of health will look for a clean and sanitary food preparation area, adequate food, refrigeration and freezer storage, and wholesome food products. Many states require a food handling card for anyone in the facility that handles food, whether it be the kitchen staff or classroom teachers.

The department of health also concerns itself with sanitation in general and determines whether a child care facility is in good sanitary condition. This includes a review of indoor and outdoor equipment and bathroom facilities. They often require plans to be submitted to them for kitchen facilities and/or the entire child care operation. Those areas of the country that have their own water treatment facilities, such as septic tanks, may face additional health department regulations.

THE FIRE DEPARTMENT

The primary concern of the fire department is the safety and welfare of children specifically relating to fire hazards, fire prevention, evacuation, and notification of the department in case of emergencies. The department may also regulate exit lighting, emergency lighting, plus the location and availability of fire extinguishers. Many localities have adopted the National Fire Prevention Code, while others still follow their own specific codes. A careful check of your local fire prevention code is the only way to clearly understand which rules and regulations your local fire prevention agency mandates you follow.

Quite often, child care centers are required to install fire alarm notification systems tied directly to the fire department or via a local alarm company.

ZONING DEPARTMENT

The zoning department in your city or county may also have regulatory capacity over child care facilities. Many communities have existing zoning ordinances for use of properties within their districts. Ordinances may dictate child care centers only be permitted in industrial and commercial areas. Centers may be an allowed use in certain types of residential areas, but not others. In some cases, where child care is not an allowed use, an appeal process or issuance of a special use permit can be pursued.

BUILDING DEPARTMENT

The building department may be involved with the regulatory process, particularly if you are building or remodeling your center. Generally, the building department requires that design plans be submitted to them for review and approval. Plans will need to cover design for parking, classroom space, playground space, and type of construction. In the case of remodeling an existing building, the department usually requires a review of plans. Ordinarily, personnel within the agency are familiar with the codes established for child care facilities and will require that plans reflect compliance with those codes.

LOCAL GOVERNMENT

Individual localities may require that other agencies or divisions under the jurisdiction of their local government have input into the establishment of a child care center. Most cities require a use permit for business, often called a business or use permit. In order not to be blindsided by regulations of an obscure agency, you are encouraged to check with them beforehand and make sure all of the necessary licenses and permits are secured.

Regulatory Checklist

[ ] Have you secured and reviewed a copy of your state's rules and regulations?

[ ] Have you clarified any rules and regulations you do not understand?

[ ] Have you determined what other agencies have regulatory authority concerning your operation?

[ ] The health department

[ ] The fire department
[ ] The zoning department
[ ] The building department
[ ] Other local agencies
[ ] Have you secured all necessary licenses, permits, and variances as a result of these contacts?

State Licensing Agencies

ALASKA
Department of Health and Social Services
Division of Family and Youth Services
P.O. Box H-05
Juneau, AK 99811-0630
(907) 465-3206

ALABAMA
Department of Human Resources
Division of Day Care and Child Development
Administrative Building
64 North Union Street
Montgomery, AL 36130
(205) 261-5785

ARKANSAS
Department of Social Services
Child Development Unit
P.O. Box 1437
Little Rock, AR 72201
(501) 682-8456

ARIZONA
Arizona Department of Health Services
Child Day Care Facilities
1824 East McKinley
Phoenix, AZ 85006
(602) 258-0551

CALIFORNIA
Department of Social Services
Community Care Facilities Division
744 P Street, Mail Section 17-17
Sacramento, CA 95814
(916) 322-8538

COLORADO
Licensing Administrator
Department of Social Services
1575 Sherman Street, Room 420
Denver, CO 80203-1714
(303) 866-5958

CONNECTICUT
State Department of Human Resources
1179 Main Street
Hartford, CT 06115
(203) 556-8048/8056

Day Care Licensing
Department of Health Services
Division of Maternal and Child Health
150 Washington Street
Hartford, CT 06106
(203) 566-2575

DISTRICT OF COLUMBIA
Department of Consumer and Regulatory Affairs
614 H Street, NW, Room 1031
Washington, DC 20001
(202) 727-7822

DELAWARE
Department of Services for Children, Youth and their Families
Division of Program Support
1825 Faulkland Road
Wilmington, DE 19805-1195
(302) 633-2700

FLORIDA
Department of Health and Rehabilitative Services
Child Care Branch
1317 Winewood Boulevard
Tallahassee, FL 32301
(904) 488-1800

GEORGIA
Day Care Licensing
Office of Regulatory Services
Georgia Department of Human Resources
878 Peachtree Street, Room 607
Atlanta, GA 30309
(404) 894-5688

HAWAII
Department of Social Services and Housing
Public Welfare Division
Program Development
P.O. Box 339
Honolulu, HI 96809
(808) 548-2302

IDAHO
Child Care Coordinator
Department of Health and Welfare
Bureau of Social Services
450 West State Street
Boise, ID 83720
(208) 334-5700

ILLINOIS
Department of Children and Family Services
406 Monroe Street
Springfield, IL 62006
(217) 627-1498

INDIANA
Department of Public Welfare
Child Welfare/Social Services Division
141 South Meridian Street, 6th Floor
Indianapolis, IN 46225
(317) 232-4521

IOWA
Bureau of Adult, Children and Family Services
Department of Human Services
5th Floor
Hoover State Office Building
Des Moines, IA 50319
(515) 281-6074

KANSAS
Kansas Department of Health and Environment
Bureau of Child Care Licensing
900 Southwest Jackson, Suite 1001
Topeka, KS 66612-1290
(913) 296-1270

KENTUCKY
Division for Licensing and Regulation
275 East Main Street
CHR Building, 4th Floor East
Frankfort, KY 40621
(502) 564-2800

LOUISIANA
Division of Licensing and Certification
Department of Health and Human Resource
P.O. Box 3767
Baton Rouge, LA 70821-3767

MAINE
Licensing Unit for Day Care
Bureau of Social Services
221 State Street
State House, Station 11
Augusta, ME 04333
(207) 289-5060

MARYLAND
Department of Child Care Licensing and Regulation
600 East Lombard Street
Baltimore, MD 21201
(301) 333-8049

Department of Health and Mental Hygiene
Family Health
201 West Preston Street
Baltimore, MD 21201
(301) 225-6743

MASSACHUSETTS
Day Care Licensing
Office for Children
10 West Street
Boston, MA 02111
(617) 727-8900

MICHIGAN
Michigan Department of Social Services
Child Day Care Licensing Division
300 South Capital
P.O. Box 30037
Lansing, MI 48909
(517) 373-8300

MINNESOTA
Division of Licensing
Department of Human Services
444 Lafayette Road
Saint Paul, MN 55155-3842
(612) 296-3971

MISSISSIPPI
Child Care and Special Licensing
Bureau of Personal Health Services
State Board of Health
P.O. Box 1700
Jackson, MS 39205
(601) 960-7740

MISSOURI
Missouri Department of Social Services
Division of Family Services
Broadway State Office Building
P.O. Box 88
Jefferson City, MO 65103
(314) 751-2450

MONTANA
Department of Family Services
P.O. Box 8005
Helena, MT 59604
(406) 444-5900

NEBRASKA
Department of Social Services
P.O. Box 95026
Lincoln, NE 68509-5026
(402) 471-3121

NEVADA
Nevada Bureau of Child Care Services
Department of Human Resources
Kindead Building
505 East King Street, Suite 606
Carson City, NV 89710
(702) 885-5911

NEW HAMPSHIRE
Bureau of Child Care Standards and Licensing
Division of Public Health Services
Health and Welfare Building, Hazen Drive
Concord, NH 03301
(603) 271-4624

NEW JERSEY
Division of Youth and Family Services
Bureau of Licensing
New Jersey Department of Social Services
1 South Montgomery Street
Trenton, NJ 08625-0717
(609) 292-1018

NEW MEXICO
Public Health Division
Licensing Bureau and Certification
Health and Environment Department
1190 St. Francis Drive
Runnels Boulevard, Suite 1350 N
Santa Fe, NM 87503
(505) 827-2444

NEW YORK
New York State Department of Social Services
Day Care Unit
40 North Pearl Street
Albany, NY 12243
(518) 473-1004

NEW YORK CITY
Bureau of Day Care
New York City Department of Health
65 Worth Street, 4th Floor
New York, NY 10013
(212) 334-7712

NORTH CAROLINA
Division of Facility Services
Child Day Care Section
701 Barbour
Raleigh, NC 27603
(919) 733-4801

NORTH DAKOTA
North Dakota Department of Human Services
Children and Family Services
State Capitol
Bismarck, ND 58505
(701) 224-4809

OHIO
Ohio Department of Human Services
Child Care Services
State Office Tower, 30th Floor, Sec. E & F
30 East Broad Street
Columbus, OH 43266-0423

OKLAHOMA
Department of Human Services
P.O. Box 25352
Oklahoma City, OK 73125
(405) 521-3561

OREGON
Children's Services Division
Department of Human Resources
198 Commercial Street, Southeast
Salem, OR 97310
(503) 378-3178

PENNSYLVANIA
Day Care Division
Department of Public Welfare
Office of Policy Planning and Evaluation
P.O. Box 2675
Harrisburg, PA 17105
(717) 783-6196

PUERTO RICO
Department of Social Services
Services to Families with Children
P.O. Box 11398
Santurce, PR 00910
(809) 724-0303

RHODE ISLAND
Rhode Island Department for Children
and Their Families
Licensing Day Care Services
610 Mount Pleasant Avenue
Providence, RI 02908
(401) 457-4536

SOUTH CAROLINA
South Carolina Department of Social Services
DCD Regulatory Unit
P.O. Box 1520
Columbia, SC 29202-9988
(803) 734-5740

SOUTH DAKOTA
Department of Social Services
Office of Child Protection Services
Richard F. Kneip Building
700 Governor Drive
Pierre, SD 57501-2291
(605) 773-3227

TENNESSEE
Department of Human Services
Licensing Unit
400 Deaderick Street
Nashville, TN 37219
(615) 741-7129

TEXAS
Texas Department of Human Resources
Licensing Division
P.O. Box 15995
Austin, TX 78761
(512) 835-2350

UTAH
Department of Social Services
Day Care Licensing
120 North Temple "200 West"
Salt Lake City, UT 84103
(801) 538-4242

VERMONT
Department of Social and Rehabilitation Services
Division of Licensing and Regulation—Day Care
103 South Main Street, 2nd Floor Osgood Boulevard
Waterbury, VT 05676
(802) 241-2158

VIRGINIA
Department of Social Services
Division of Licensing Programs
Blair Building
8007 Discovery Drive
Richmond, VA 23229-8699
(804) 281-9025

VIRGIN ISLANDS
Bureau of Day Care Service
Department of Social Welfare
P.O. Box 550
Charlotte Amalie
Saint Thomas, VI 00801
(809) 774-4570

WASHINGTON
Department of Social and Health Services
Division of Children and Family Services
OB-41 D
Olympia, WA 98504
(206) 753-0614

WEST VIRGINIA
Department of Human Services
Division of Social Services
1900 Washington Street, East
Charleston, WV 25305
(304) 348-7980

WISCONSIN
Wisconsin Department of Health and Social Services
Office for Children, Youth and Families
Division of Community Services
1 West Wilson Street
P.O. Box 7851
Madison, WI 53707
(608) 266-8200

WYOMING
Division of Public Assistance and Social Services
Family Services
Hathaway Building
Cheyenne, WY 82002
(307) 777-6285

4

Determining Your
Organizational Structure

As with any business, opening and running a child care center demands a well-defined organizational plan. There are two main subgroups relating to organizational structure: nonprofit and proprietary, meaning privately owned and managed. A nonprofit organization must incorporate as such. An organization that is proprietary can fall into many subgroups: sole proprietorship, partnership, corporation, or sub chapter S corporation.

Nonprofit Organizations

Child care can be regarded as an educational function and, as such, is eligible for nonprofit status. There are many steps involved with forming a nonprofit, tax-exempt organization. The ultimate goal—approval of 501(C)(3) tax exempt status—is contingent upon you meeting many qualifications, one of which is to form a board of directors.

The board of directors is the governing body of a nonprofit organization. These organizations are generally administered by a paid staff. In addition, they may pay appropriate salaries and other expenses incurred in the day-to-day running of the business. They also may accept payments for the services they render.

It is important to note that a major difference between the nonprofit and proprietary organization is in its method of compensation. The director of a nonprofit child care center is compensated for his or her work with an established salary. The owners of a proprietary business receive compensation from profits generated.

A nonprofit status brings with it a number of advantages other than tax exemption. There are government programs available for nonprofits in the form of grants or subsidies. These include the U.S. Department of Agriculture's Food Program, which offers reimbursement for nutritious meals and snacks offered to children in child care facilities. A proprietary child care center may participate in the USDA Food Program provided they meet specific guidelines.

Proprietary Organizations

The National Child Care Association estimates there are over 50,000 child care centers in the United States operating on a for-profit basis. The *Wall Street Journal* reports child care business is luring entrepreneurs in increasing numbers.

The child care industry has recently seen the rapid growth of national chains of child care centers. The larger of these chains have over 100 centers each. Mid-sized chains of child care centers have also experienced a mushrooming growth pattern. There are, however, less than 50 of these mid-sized chains. These companies operate child care facilities on a regional, multi-state, and single-state basis. The majority started as single center operations. They have expanded their enterprises because parents were satisfied with their child care services, and the individual entrepreneurs at the helm had the energy and the working capital to expand.

Proprietary centers have several options when considering their organizational structure. These structures take the form of sole proprietorships, partnerships, and corporations.

Sole Proprietorships

With the sole proprietorship option one person controls the business. He or she retains all responsibility and decision-making power. As such, this individual typically commits to financing the operation via personal resources or through personal credit, conceptualizing and organizing the entire plan, then carrying it out. The sole proprietor also has the responsibility to claim on their personal income tax returns all the income and all the expenses related to the business. The obvious advantage to sole proprietorship is that total autonomy and control remains in the hands of the individual.

A sole proprietor may choose to establish some type of advisory board for the purpose of seeking advice and input. According to the sole proprietor's needs, this can be designed as a parent advisory board, a staff advisory board, or an academic advisory board.

Partnerships

A partnership is formed when two or more individuals act as partners to establish and run a business operation. There is no limit to the number of partners who can engage in activity in a partnership, although the larger the number, the more appealing the corporate alternative becomes. In a partnership, there must be a very clear definition of the duties and responsibilities of each partner.

Financial partners or "backers"—those individuals who help finance the operation—are often involved in the ownership base as a partner, many times as silent partners. Financial partners may not have expertise in the field or be interested in the day-to-day operations of the business. The silent partner's involvement is strictly financial. So, too, is the return. The importance of financial backers cannot be understated—they often are the people who can get the operation off the ground and running.

In the case of active partners, it is important that their roles and responsibilities within the organization is clearly defined. Many business advisors counsel their clients on the hazards of establishing partnerships. The old cliche that friends and business just don't mix often holds true. By clearly defining roles, you help prevent misunderstanding and potential conflict and ensure to some degree that the partnership effort is successful.

In establishing roles for partners it is important to take into consideration each person's expertise and skills. If one partner is a financial wizard, the role of maintaining and keeping the records should be placed in his or her hands. Another partner may have skills in the area of marketing and public relations. Those tasks should be assigned to that individual.

Business consultants often advise those who are in the process of forming partnerships to establish a written plan and policies to guide them in the successful operation of their business. In addition, a plan of dissolution should be drawn up so that, if circumstances change and a termination of the partnership is desired, a mechanism already in place to make the change smooth and efficient.

Individuals involved in a child care center partnership must also declare their share of the income and expenses of the operation on their individual tax returns. It should be noted that partnerships often vary in their percentage of ownership. If two people are interested in forming a business partnership, they may choose to establish a 50/50 division. If, however, one partner has invested less than another in the business, the percentage basis might be 80/20. With the addition of other partners, the percentage of ownership of an individual partner can vary considerably.

Corporations

An individual or group may, for various reasons, make the decision to form a corporation for the operation of their child care enterprise. If the decision has been made to become a nonprofit entity, a corporate structure is a must. A proprietary center may choose to incorporate as well. To form a corporation you must establish officers and a board of directors; a minimum of three board members are usually needed.

Incorporation is processed through state government. The office of the secretary of state handles incorporation documents. By familiarizing yourself with state requirements for incorporation, you can prepare yourself to begin the process. It is recommended you consult with a professional tax accountant and/or an attorney during this phase, although there are books and publications that thoroughly outline the incorporation process.

Subchapter S Corporations

The Internal Revenue Service has established a special category of corporation for small businesses called a Subchapter S Corporation. Although similar to regular corporate status, there are significant differences. Consultation with a knowledgeable professional is advised.

Most industry analysts expect the child care industry to expand as the demand for services increases. The larger and mid-sized chains will more than likely grow at a faster rate than single center operations. It is anticipated, however, that the individual entrepreneur involved in providing child care for America's children in center facilities will remain the driving force in the industry.

5

Handling Money Matters

Start-up

During the start-up phase of opening a child care center, a projected budget in the form of a spreadsheet must be developed. This involves two major components: the projected revenue /income and projected expenses.

In the start-up phase of a business enterprise, the initial projected revenues are those funds generated specifically for start-up costs—whether they are individual investments, funds from a granting source or lending institution, or a combination of the above.

It is critically important for anyone planning to open a child care center to determine that these initial sources of capital are adequate to cover initial expenses. As the business enterprise becomes established and begins serving clients and generating income, the funds are then considered to be on-going revenue. It is equally important to determine whether or not sources of on-going income will be enough to cover on-going expenses.

Without a clear picture of your projected budget, your chances for success are limited. The Small Business Administration (SBA) estimates over 80% of new businesses fail within the first year because they lack sufficient capital. The SBA also estimates over 90% of these failures occur as a result of poor planning.

The primary sources of revenue for most child care programs are the fees paid for child care services rendered or tuition. For some child care programs, tuition may be the only revenue source. Others may receive additional funds from programs such as the USDA Food Program, which subsidizes meals served to children in care, or Title

XX funds from the government, which assist low income families to pay for child care.

When developing your start-up budget, it is necessary to list every item that will be an expense as you begin to operate your child care center. It is vital to list every expense you will incur during the first month of operation, before receiving any tuition income. The expenses incurred in the months following that first month will be included in your projected on-going budget. To be certain you've included all of the expenses, it is necessary to design a spreadsheet of expenses.

The SBA recommends all new businesses (and even requires it of all those applying for financing through them) have this spreadsheet of expenses broken into separate categories for a 3-month period, a 6-month period, and a 12-month period.

Start-up costs should include the following categories: food and food preparation—salaries and payroll—taxes—rent, lease or mortgage payment—repairs—utilities—telephone—center supplies—advertising—insurance—office expenses—miscellaneous expenses—and other.

Initial Financial Resources

The most important consideration one has to make in starting a child care center is determining where and how you will secure the necessary financial resources. Since personal financial status varies so greatly among prospective child care operators, there are no set formulas for success here.

After carefully analyzing your personal financial situation and the financial requirements your child care enterprise demands, there are several routes you may pursue:

DOING IT ON YOUR OWN

If your personal finances are adequate to cover all expenses for opening your center and carrying it through its initial phases, consider yourself fortunate. You will need to make the necessary arrangements to have access to your existing capital as the need arises. It may seem at times like there is no end to the need for more money, but with proper planning, accurate estimates will guide you through this.

TAPPING COMMUNITY RESOURCES

Child care centers with nonprofit status may be eligible for a host of income sources including private foundation grants, corporate funding, donations, in-kind services and United Way funding.

Go to your local library and research what grants may be available to you on a local and national level. Contact the United Way organizational headquarters, your local Resource and Referral agency, volunteer organizations (such as the Junior League), service organizations (such as the Lions and Rotary Clubs), and the Small Business Administration.

DOING IT WITH PARTNERS

If you have made the decision to include financial partners in your business endeavor, proper agreements and contracts will need to be drawn up to reflect your intentions. The most appropriate action, in some instances, will be to form a partnership. In other instances, it may be more appropriate to form a corporate structure.

If the inclusion of partners in your business plan is limited to one other partner, and your percentage of ownership is a 50/50 split, then your agreement is fairly straightforward. If the inclusion of partners involves multiple people, a clear definition of ownership percentage is necessary and important.

Another factor to consider in addition to ownership is the clear definition of role and duty. Many partnerships falter because roles are unclear and responsibilities are not shared according to expectation.

Financial participation may also be in the form of a corporation with each of the investing corporate stockholders purchasing a proportionate share of stock to the amount they have invested. In the case of multiple partners, this is often the recommended course of action. Consultation with a business advisor and/or attorney is recommended to clarify these points and avoid future problems.

DOING IT WITH THE BANK

If your personal financial situation dictates investment by an outside party, such as a bank or lending institution, you will need to follow the appropriate application procedures established by that lending institution. A sample loan application form is included for your review.

The following categories should be considered when creating your spreadsheet of expenses.

Food and Food Preparation

This category should include all necessary staple food products and include everything needed to equip the kitchen to make it ready for food preparation. In some instances, this may include the major appliances needed for a good working kitchen: a stove, sink (three compartment sinks are needed in some areas), refrigerator, dishwasher, possibly a microwave oven, and food preparation surfaces such as tables or counters.

In some instances, the cost for these major items may be included in the cost of your building space, whether it be a lease or a purchase. Other miscellaneous items needed to equip the kitchen include utensils, pots and pans, serving bowls and equipment, silverware and dinnerware. There are also basic food staples needed in every kitchen for continual food preparation. These items are the stocked shelf items, such as flour, sugar, and spices.

You should contact several food and restaurant supply companies as prices vary greatly. They even fluctuate from one week to the next. Depending on your purchase arrangements, the quantity of food necessary to run your program, and the amount of storage space available, you may choose to order your food products on a weekly, bi-weekly, or monthly basis. Perishables need to be purchased on a more frequent basis than canned or boxed items. Take advantage of sales and stock up if you can afford it.

This food and food preparation category should also include your initial supply of milk and dairy products. Please note that some localities require a separate refrigerated milk dispenser.

Shop comparatively with several dairy companies in your area to choose the most cost effective means of purchasing. Milk and milk products are an important part of a center's nutrition program and will consequently be a fairly substantial item on the expense sheet.

Payroll

The next category on your start up spreadsheet should be payroll. In a child care facility, payroll costs will ordinarily exceed any other individual category on the list of expenses.   Determine what key staff is needed prior to your actual opening date. You may decide the director and other administrative personnel should be hired prior to the center opening to coordinate your public relations and marketing plans, as well as building and classroom preparation.

In addition, teachers may be needed for a short period prior to the opening to arrange classrooms and prepare for the first day of activity. You may decide additional people, such as kitchen help, maintenance crew, and drivers are needed for several days of training.

It is necessary to prepare a work sheet of those activities you will need to engage in prior to your opening date; identify what staff will be assigned to complete those activities.

In determining what your start-up and ongoing payroll expenses will be, "survey" other local child care facilities to gauge the going rate of pay. Then as you negotiate with potential employees, you will have a clear picture of what is currently being offered in the marketplace. You may find that to attract key people for employment it is necessary to pay a slightly higher salary base. You may discover, however, you are on such a tight budget it is impossible for you to pay a higher salary base, and you need to appeal to potential employees in other ways. Alternative compensation might include child care at a reduced rate, training, or educational opportunities paid for by the child-care facility.

Prior to the first payroll, it is necessary to apply for an Employer Identification Number (EIN) with the Internal Revenue Service and with your state and local taxing authorities. This application will automatically place you on a mailing list to receive the proper forms for compliance with withholding tax laws.

When you apply for an EIN, you will also receive notification from the Internal Revenue Service of workshops conducted for new business owners and employers. These workshops serve to inform you of the necessary steps you must take in processing a payroll.

In setting up a payroll system, you may choose to use the services of an accountant or payroll service. Tax laws and withholding laws have become more complicated over the last few years and this trend will probably continue. Professional advice could be a wise investment.

Taxes

Next on your start-up expense sheet is taxes. This column can be handled in several different ways. One approach is to include any and all tax amounts and other fees paid to governmental agencies. Another approach is to include all payroll taxes under the payroll category and include only those other incidental taxes and governmental fees in this tax column. These fees will include such items as licensing, ownership registrations, and personal property taxes.

In the start-up phase of your operation, you will incur some one-time fee expenses. Others—such as property taxes, employment taxes, and head taxes—will also be on-going expenses.

Rent/Lease/Purchase

Start-up expense in this category should be easy to project. Whatever rent, lease, or purchase arrangements you have made, any expenses incurred in making those arrangements would be included in this column. Be sure to include such items as security deposits, common area maintenance fees, loan fees, escrow costs or any sign fees to which you may have agreed.

In negotiating a lease with a property owner or a property management company, it is important to remember that you are agreeing to a long-term contract. Your initial negotiation will have lasting fiscal impact for your operation.

Many child care operators have negotiated favorable lease terms which include graduated increases in lease payments. You may attempt to negotiate a reduced lease payment or no lease payment for the period prior to the initial opening of your center when no tuition income can be realized. Months may be spent in the renovation process, and a reduced or no lease payment can add up to substantial savings.

Most property management companies and property owners are in the business of leasing property. You are in the business of child care. You may wish to seek the advice of others in negotiating a lease arrangement prior to its signing. It is always wise to have an attorney review any lease document before you sign it. Although this may seem awkward, better to have professional counsel now than to find a flaw in a lease agreement you have already signed.

The rent/lease entry on your start-up expense sheet should also reflect security deposits, earnest money, and any other costs included in the lease arrangement. If renovations need to be made to a building or property, try to include these costs in your lease negotiations. In many instances, if a tenant is willing to sign a long-term lease agreement, the cost of renovations can be included as part of the negotiated deal.

Since renovations can be quite costly, this option is worth pursuing. If it is necessary, however, to accept the financial responsibility for renovations, these items need to be included in your start-up expense sheet.

Another option is entering into a purchase agreement rather than a rent/lease agreement. In this case payments are usually made in the form of installment mortgage payments. These payments are entered in a separate category on your spreadsheet as "other expenses." A professional should be consulted regarding the deductibility for tax purposes of this type of expense.

Your local community may require you to submit design plans. Careful consideration should be given to any and all expenses that will be incurred in developing these plans.

Repairs and Maintenance

Repairs and maintenance should be listed as a separate line item on the start-up expense sheet.

Repairs to major equipment such as heating, ventilating, and air conditioning systems (HVAC), can be expensive when you negotiate your lease arrangement. If, for example, you know the equipment is old and may be in need of repair, insist on an initial inspection to evaluate the condition.

In some lease arrangements, it may be the designated responsibility of the landlord to keep these systems in running order. In case after case, there have been instances of everything working perfectly well until you are responsible for it.

Utilities

Start-up expenses in the utilities category vary greatly in amount. When we think of utilities, gas and electricity immediately come to mind. Don't forget to include the expense of start-up costs for both of these services. In most instances, this requires a deposit with the utility company until you have established a satisfactory payment record. In some localities, this may mean a prepayment of the estimated first month's charges. Other utilities to take into consideration are water and sewer.

Telephone

Telephone systems have become quite complex and expensive in recent years. Determine what type of telephone service and equipment your center will require. There are free professional consultants in the communications field who can help you find a system to meet your needs. Initial start-up costs for telephone service can be substantial. Contact your local telephone company for an accurate estimate of initial costs.

If alterations of telephone lines are needed, additional expenses can be incurred. You will need to decide whether to lease or purchase your telephone equipment. This is an individual decision, but keep in mind the amount of equipment you need, cost involved, on-going maintenance of the equipment, and the potential for upgrading your system.

Supplies and Equipment

Supplies and equipment are a substantial expense in the start-up of your business. Those items that are a must on a start-up spreadsheet include: furniture and fixtures, playground equipment, classroom supplies, activity center materials, paper and other disposable products, cleaning and janitorial supplies, and other necessary equipment. For major items, be sure to get the highest quality you can afford so the equipment will last.

There are a number of office and teacher supply companies throughout the country, so shop around to find the best value. More than one child care program has found garage sales, flea markets, and clearance sales to be a prime source of much needed equipment.

Advertising

Advertising is another line item on an expense sheet. As a child care center operator, you may choose to do a considerable amount of advertising prior to the opening of your center. Advertising strategies vary greatly in price. Costs for advertising might include printing and distribution of fliers, brochures, banners, directory listings, newspaper advertising, and special events.

Insurance

Initial expenses incurred for insurance coverage should be included in your start-up spreadsheet. Your insurance carrier may require a down payment that is a portion of your annual premium.

Consideration should be given to all types of insurance needed and the expense involved in those coverages. Do not forget to include general liability, property coverages, automobile insurance, medical insurance, life insurance, accidental medical insurance, directors and officers liability, workman's compensation insurance, and umbrella policies.

Office

Office expenses include: printed forms, bookkeeping systems, stationery, business cards, handbooks, and other day-to-day office supplies.

Miscellaneous Expenses

Miscellaneous expenses include all of those items that don't readily fit in another category and yet are true business expenses.

Other Expenses

Expenses can generally be considered as "other" if they are not tax deductible as a business expense. For example, if a purchase arrangement is made for the location of your program and a mortgage is paid rather than a lease payment, that mortgage payment can be listed in this other expenses category and may be included in a discretionary category. An accountant can give you more detailed information on tax deductible expenses.

Balance Sheet

From this spreadsheet of expenses, you can then draw up a balance sheet. A balance sheet simply lists on one side all the expenses incurred for various reasons and purposes and on the other side lists all income. An initial balance sheet will give you the facts in black and white as to whether your anticipated sources of revenue for start-up can meet anticipated line item expenses.

Budget Projections

In starting any business, it's necessary to do a projection sheet so you can forecast what the future holds for your burgeoning business. A projection sheet should be drawn up on a monthly basis for an interval period of at least one year. (A sample is included in this book.) Please remember that it takes time for a business to get off the ground and for an educational program to become successful. Overnight success, although not unheard of, is unusual.

Your projection sheet should include all the line items listed in the spreadsheet. It also needs to include detailed information about projected enrollments and projected revenues. The start-up spreadsheet gives you itemized details of all of your expenses up to day one. Your projection sheet should start at that point. Since the growing size of your enrollment will correlate directly with income and expenses, start with that item.

Although projections are referred to as simply guesswork, try to make them as educated a guess as possible. After talking with people about advertising concepts and getting a general feel in the area where your program will begin, do a projected estimate of how many children you will have in your first month. You may want to break this down into program components, such as infant, toddler, preschool, pre-kindergarten, and school-age children. Or you may want to treat it as one total number depending on the type and size of your program. With this projected enrollment number in mind, you need to forecast the income you will garner from that enrollment.

For example, if you project that in your first month of operation you will have three infants and your weekly income for infant care is $130 per child, then you can safely project you will have an income of $390 per week for your infant program. If you multiply that times the 4.33 average weeks in a month, the result will be an estimate of what your income will be from that infant program.

Likewise with toddlers. If you reasonably project you will have five toddlers in your first month and your toddler rate is set at $105 per week, then you can project your monthly income will be $525 for your toddler program. Multiply that times 4.33, and you end up with an estimate of the revenue to be generated by your toddler program in its first month of operation.

The same process applies for all other age groups in classroom categories in your program. Although this system seems rather straightforward and overly simplified, the following considerations need to be taken into account:

- Special discounts you give for new enrollments may decrease your revenue at first.
- Absences can impact your revenue. Your absence policy will dictate how absences will affect your revenue base from a given enrollment.
- You may choose to enroll part-time students. Depending on the rate structure established for part-time enrollments, this can affect your revenue base greatly.

Once you have established a projected enrollment base for your program, you may then go through the line items in your spreadsheet and fill in projected amounts for those expenses. Beginning with the first item in the sample spreadsheet, food and preparation, it is easy to see that the number of students enrolled in your program will have a great bearing on the expense of food and preparation. If projected enrollment in your first month is twenty students, you will then be able to purchase the necessary food supplies to feed twenty students. If, however, your projected enrollment is forty students, it becomes necessary to double your food purchasing requirements. Although the cost involved may not double because of the economy of scale, it certainly will increase.

The next expense item on the spreadsheet, payroll, is directly proportionate to your projected enrollment. For example, if your first monthly projected enrollment is twenty students, it will be necessary for you to staff appropriately for twenty students. If, however, your projected enrollment for the first month is forty students, you can see that your projected staffing requirements will be doubled. And your projected payroll expense item will also be doubled.

Although the other items on the spreadsheet's projection may not have as great a correlation to the actual enrollment, they do have some relationship. Therefore, the amounts you enter in your projection sheet for those other line items should be calculated carefully. For example, the lease payment for the space used for your child care program may have a direct relation to the number of children enrolled or revenue generated in the business operation. Many leases are negotiated containing factors such as these. However, other leases are set up on a flat-rate basis, and regardless of enrollment or income/ revenue generated, the lease payment remains the same. In the case of a purchased property, the amount paid for an amortized mortgage contract will remain the same.

Another example of this variability is in utilities. At first glance, a utility payment may be viewed as a fixed expense. However, in starting up a program, if enrollment is somewhat lower than the capacity your space would allow, then it's possible some of this unused space may be shut off and utility service to that area minimized.

Because of the variability in the line items of a projection sheet, it is necessary to do a careful projection on a month-to-month basis for an initial period. Completing a detailed projection sheet with both income and expenses on a monthly basis will allow you to do a projected balance sheet on a monthly basis. This balance sheet is your barometer as to the success of your program. Naturally, it can be expected that the balance sheet will be negative for a given amount of time.

In the world of doing business, a positive balance sheet is always the goal. Many variables enter into the picture of positive and negative balance sheets, especially at the inception of a business. Some child care center providers have expressed alarm at not having a positive balance sheet on opening day of business. Others have expressed concern about not having a positive balance sheet after three or even six months. And yet other child care center operators feel quite accomplished if after a six or twelve month period their child care center is operating in the black. The time of year you choose to open your center, the location, and the proximity of other programs all enter into the picture of projected success.

Reality Sets In

After careful analysis of a start-up budget and careful consideration of a projected budget, you can make a well-informed decision as to the potential for success of your plan to operate a child care facility. If, after all the financial facts are clearly identified, the potential for success looks bleak, you need to go back to the drawing board. Determine where the flaws in the plan are, if they can be corrected, and in what way. This is where your own individual savvy and that of your other business advisors (accountants, attorneys, and other professionals in the child care field) can assist you in determining your level of risk. All entrepreneurs share one common denominator. They are risk takers. The question then arises, at what level of risk do you as an individual feel comfortable.

After all is said and done, if you choose to open your child care program, a redo of each of the monthly spreadsheets needs to be done with actual figures rather than projected ones. This becomes the spreadsheet of actual business operation. Each of the expense items listed earlier needs to be addressed as to what actual expenses were incurred in that category. Once this is accomplished, you will have the necessary information to do a detailed financial analysis of the success or failure of your operation on a monthly basis.

A comparison with the projected budget is very important. This comparative analysis allows you to determine if your projection is on track or totally off base. If you determine your projection is on track, this tells your future projections are more than likely correct as well. If, however, you find a considerable disparity between the actual spreadsheet and the projected spreadsheet, you need to re-evaluate your initial projections. Sometimes projection sheets are done so cautiously and so conservatively that the actual figures are better. In this case, a re-evaluation of the projections would permit you to scale your projections upward in a positive manner. If, however, the opposite occurs and you find your projection was overly optimistic, you will need to scale down your anticipated business activity on your financial sheet. Take a more realistic look at the ramifications that such a scale down will bring.

Spreadsheet Example

MAJOR SPREADSHEET LINE ITEMS

Name	Date/	Ch. #		Amt.		Food		Payroll		Taxes		Rent		Repairs	
Watts-Hardy Milk	12/2	159	01	100	00	100	00								
CCCOC	X		03	12	00					12	00				
School Supply USA	X		04	300	00										
PSC	12/1	159	22	200	00										
Mtn Bell	12/4		37	300	00										
CS	12/2		38	416	76			116	76						
ND	X		39	264	62			264	62						
CS	12/15		66	116	76			116	76						
ND	X		67	322	08			322	08						
Sullivan	12/8	159	80	124	76									124	76
D Hoover	12/15		81	388	00									388	00
Burg Ins.	X		82	185	84										
Lindyo (N/A)	12/26	160	18	46	64										
ND	12/29	160	19	320	33			320	33						
Corner Mkt.	12/29	160	22	100	00	100	00								
Globe Properties	X	160	43	500	00							500	00		
Petersons (Mtg.)	X		44	1124	67										
Total				4521	96	200	00	1140	55	12	00	5000	00	512	76

Spreadsheet Example

Name	Utilities		Phone		Supplies		Advert.		Ins.		Office		Other		Other Pymt.	
Watts-Hardy Milk CCCOC School Supply USA PSC Mtn Bell	200	00	300	00	300	00										
CS ND CS ND Sullivan																
D Hoover Burg Ins. Lindyo (N/A) ND Corner Mkt.									183	54	46	64				
Globe Properties Petersons (Mtg.)															1124	67
Total	200	00	300	00	300	00			183	54	46	64			1124	67

Securing a Loan

So that we may best serve your banking needs, please provide the Information requested. Be sure to read these instructions and check the appropriate box or boxes before completing this application.

Instructions:

Checking and Savings Accounts

[ ] If you are applying for a checking or savings account in your own name, complete Section A only.

[ ] If you are applying for a joint checking or savings account, complete both Sections A and B.

Guaranteed Check Card, On-Line Reserve or Consumer Loan

[ ] If you are applying for credit in your own name and are relying exclusively on your own income or assets as the basis for repayment, complete Sections A and C only.

[ ] If you are applying for joint credit, complete all sections.

[ ] If you are applying for credit in your own name, but relying on income from alimony, child support, or separate maintenance or on the income or assets of another person as the basis for repayment, complete all sections to the extent possible. Provide information in Section B about the person on whose alimony, child support, or maintenance payments or income or assets you are relying.

Date _____

Section A—Information About You as an Applicant

Your Full Name (First, Middle and Last)		Birthdate	No. of Dependents
Your Street Address		Home Phone ( )	
City, State and Zip		County	How Long — Years Months
Driver's License No. and State	Other Identification	Social Security Number	
Previous Street Address		City, State and Zip	
Employer	Type of Business	Occupation or Position	How Long — Years Months
Employer's Street Address		City, State and Zip	Business Phone ( )
Previous Employer	Address	Occupation or Position	How Long — Years Months
Name of Nearest Relative Not Living With You		Relationship	
Relative's Street Address		City, State and Zip	Relative's Phone ( )
Do you presently have accounts at any other bank. ☐ Yes Specify: ☐ No			
Former Bank		Address	

Section B—Information About Joint Applicant or Other Person

Full Name (First, Middle and Last)		Birthdate
Street Address		Home Phone ( )
City, State and Zip		County
Driver's License No. and State	Other Identification	Social Security Number
Employer	Type of Business	Occupation or Position How Long — Years Months
Employer's Street Address	City, State and Zip	Business Phone ( )
Previous Employer	Address	Occupation or Position How Long — Years Months
Name of Nearest Relative	Relationship	Relative's Phone ( )
Relative's Street Address	City, State and Zip	

Securing a Loan

Section C—Financial Information (to be completed only if you are applying for credit)

Complete this section giving information about you. If applicable (see instructions at the beginning of this application), include information about the joint applicant or other person.

I am applying for: ☐ Guaranteed Check Card   ☐ Consumer Loan

Amount Requested $	Purpose of Loan (Specify if applying for Consumer Loan)

Account Information

		Income: You do not have to reveal income from alimony, child support, or separate maintenance unless you wish to have it considered as a basis for repayment.		
Checking Account Number	Bank Name and Address			
		Description	Gross Amount	Net Take Home Pay
Checking Account Number	Bank Name and Address	Your Monthly Income Primary Job	$	$
Savings Account Number	Financial Institution and Address	Other Income (Specify)	$	$
Savings Account Number	Financial Institution and Address	Joint Applicant or Other Person's Income Primary Job	$	$
Home Please check regarding your home ▶ ☐ Own ☐ Rent ☐ Mortgage ☐ Contract	Yr. Purch. / Purchase Price $ / Present Market Value $	Joint Applicant or Other Person's Other Income (Specify)	$	$
		Total Income ▶	$	$

	Address	Monthly Payment or Rent	Balance Due
1st Mortgage Holder or Landlord	Address	$	$
2nd Mortgage Holder	Address	Monthly Payment $	Balance Due $
Auto (Year, Make and Model)	Insurance Company and Agent		
Auto Financed By	Address	Monthly Payment $	Balance Due $
2nd Auto (Year, Make and Model)	Insurance Company and Agent		
Auto Financed By	Address	Monthly Payment $	Balance Due $
Other Loan (Lender's Name)	Address	Monthly Payment $	Balance Due $
Other Loan (Lender's Name)	Address	Monthly Payment $	Balance Due $
Other Loan (Lender's Name)	Address	Monthly Payment $	Balance Due $
Master Charge Number	Name of Bank and Location	Monthly Payment $	Balance Due $
Visa Number	Address	Monthly Payment $	Balance Due $
Other Charge Account and Number	Address	Monthly Payment $	Balance Due $
Other Charge Account and Number	Address	Monthly Payment $	Balance Due $
Other Charge Account and Number	Address	Monthly Payment $	Balance Due $
Other Charge Account and Number	Address	Monthly Payment $	Balance Due $
Other Obligations (Examples: Insurance Payments, Medical Bills, Liability to Pay Alimony, Child Support or Separate Maintenance).	Specify	Monthly Payments $	Balances Due $
Have you ever been a subject of a Bankruptcy proceeding or are there any unsatisfied judgments against you? Describe:	Totals ▶	$	$

Everything that I have stated in this application is correct to the best of my knowledge. I understand that _____ will retain this application whether or not it is approved. I authorize the bank to check my credit and employment history and to answer future questions about its credit experience with me.

X _____   X _____
Your Signature   **Date**   **Joint Applicant's Signature (If Applicable)**   **Date**

Payroll taxes

Form **941**	**Employer's Quarterly Federal Tax Return**
(Rev. January 1989) Department of the Treasury Internal Revenue Service	**4141** ▶ For Paperwork Reduction Act Notice, see page 2. Please type or print.

Your name, address, employer identification number, and calendar quarter of return. (If not correct, please change.)

▶

Name (as distinguished from trade name)   Date quarter ended

Trade name, if any   Employer identification number

Address and ZIP code

OMB No. 1545-0029
Expires: 5-31-91

T

FF

FD

FP

I

T

If address is different from prior return, check here ▶ ☐

IRS Use

1 1 1 1 1 1 1 1 1 1   2   3 3 3 3 3 3   4 4 4

5 5 5   6   7   8 8 8 8 8 8   9 9 9   10 10 10 10 10 10 10 10 10

If you do not have to file returns in the future, check here . . . ▶ ☐   Date final wages paid . . . . ▶

If you are a seasonal employer, see **Seasonal employer** on page 2 and check here . . . ▶ ☐

1a Number of employees (except household) employed in the pay period that includes March 12th . ▶	**1a**	
b If you are a subsidiary corporation AND your parent corporation files a consolidated Form 1120, enter parent corporation employer identification number (EIN) . . ▶ **1b** –		
2 Total wages and tips subject to withholding, plus other compensation . . . . ▶	**2**	
3 Total income tax withheld from wages, tips, pensions, annuities, sick pay, gambling, etc. . . . ▶	**3**	
4 Adjustment of withheld income tax for preceding quarters of calendar year (see instructions) . . ▶	**4**	
5 Adjusted total of income tax withheld (see instructions)	**5**	
6 Taxable social security wages paid . . . . . $ _____|_____ × 15.02% (.1502) .	**6**	
7a Taxable tips reported . . . . $ _____|_____ × 15.02% (.1502) .	**7a**	
b Taxable hospital insurance wages paid . . . . $ _____|_____ × 2.9% (.029). . .	**7b**	
8 Total social security taxes (add lines 6, 7a, and 7b)	**8**	
9 Adjustment of social security taxes (see instructions for required explanation)	**9**	
10 Adjusted total of social security taxes (see instructions) . . . . ▶	**10**	
11 Backup withholding (see instructions)	**11**	
12 Adjustment of backup withholding tax for preceding quarters of calendar year . . . . . . ▶	**12**	
13 Adjusted total of backup withholding	**13**	
14 Total taxes (add lines 5, 10, and 13)	**14**	
15 Advance earned income credit (EIC) payments, if any . . . . ▶	**15**	
16 Net taxes (subtract line 15 from line 14). **This must equal line IV below** (plus line IV of Schedule A (Form 941) if you have treated backup withholding as a separate liability)	**16**	
17 Total deposits for quarter, including overpayment applied from a prior quarter, from your records . ▶	**17**	
18 Balance due (subtract line 17 from line 16). This should be less than $500. Pay to IRS . . . . ▶	**18**	

19 If line 17 is more than line 16, enter overpayment here ▶ $ _____ and check if to be:
☐ Applied to next return   **OR**   ☐ Refunded.

Record of Federal Tax Liability (Complete if line 16 is $500 or more.) See the instructions on page 4 for details before checking these boxes.
Check only if you made eighth-monthly deposits using the 95% rule ▶ ☐   Check only if you are a first time 3-banking-day depositor ▶ ☐

Show tax liability here, **not deposits.** IRS gets deposit data from FTD coupons.

Date wages paid	First month of quarter		Second month of quarter		Third month of quarter	
1st through 3rd	A		I		Q	
4th through 7th	B		J		R	
8th through 11th	C		K		S	
12th through 15th	D		L		T	
16th through 19th	E		M		U	
20th through 22nd	F		N		V	
23rd through 25th	G		O		W	
26th through the last	H		P		X	
Total liability for month	I		II		III	

(left margin: Do NOT Show Federal Tax Deposits Here)

▶ **IV** Total for quarter (add lines **I, II,** and **III**). **This must equal line 16 above** . . . . ▶

Sign Here   Under penalties of perjury, I declare that I have examined this return, including accompanying schedules and statements, and to the best of my knowledge and belief, it is true, correct, and complete.

Signature ▶   Title ▶   Date ▶

Payroll taxes

Form **940**	**Employer's Annual Federal Unemployment (FUTA) Tax Return**	OMB No. 1545-0028
Department of the Treasury Internal Revenue Service	▶ For Paperwork Reduction Act Notice, see page 2.	19**88**

If incorrect, make any necessary change. ▶	Name (as distinguished from trade name)	Calendar year	T
			FF
	Trade name, if any		FD
			FP
	Address and ZIP code		I
		Employer identification number	T
		—	

A Did you pay all required contributions to state unemployment funds by the due date of Form 940? (See instructions if none required.) . . . ☐ Yes ☐ No
If you checked the "Yes" box, enter the amount of contributions paid to state unemployment funds . . . . ▶ $

B Are you required to pay contributions to only one state? . . . . ☐ Yes ☐ No
If you checked the "Yes" box: (1) Enter the name of the state where you are required to pay contributions . . . . . ▶
(2) Enter your state reporting number(s) as shown on state unemployment tax return. ▶

C If any part of wages taxable for FUTA tax is exempt from state unemployment tax, check the box. (See the Specific Instructions on page 2.). . . . . ☐

Part I   Computation of Taxable Wages and Credit Reduction (to be completed by all taxpayers)

1	Total payments (including exempt payments) during the calendar year for services of employees	1	
2	Exempt payments. (Explain each exemption shown, attaching additional sheets if necessary.) ▶	Amount paid	
		2	
3	Payments for services of more than $7,000. Enter only the excess over the first $7,000 paid to individual employees not including exempt amounts shown on line 2. Do not use the state wage limitation.	3	
4	Total exempt payments (add lines 2 and 3)	4	
5	**Total taxable wages** (subtract line 4 from line 1). (If any part is exempt from state contributions, see instructions.) ▶	5	

Part II   Tax Due or Refund (Complete if you checked the "Yes" boxes in both questions A and B and did not check the box in C above.)

1	Total FUTA tax. Multiply the wages in Part I, line 5, by .008 and enter here.	1	
2	Minus: Total FUTA tax deposited for the year, including any overpayment applied from a prior year (from your records)	2	
3	**Balance due** (subtract line 2 from line 1). This should be $100 or less. Pay to IRS . . . . ▶	3	
4	**Overpayment** (subtract line 1 from line 2). Check if it is to be: ☐ Applied to next return, or ☐ Refunded . . ▶	4	

Part III   Tax Due or Refund (Complete if you checked the "No" box in either question A or B or you checked the box in C above. Also complete Part V.)

1	Gross FUTA tax. Multiply the wages in Part I, line 5, by .062	1	
2	Maximum credit. Multiply the wages in Part I, line 5, by .054	2	
3	**Credit allowable:** Enter the smaller of the amount in Part V, line 11, or Part III, line 2 . .	3	
4	Total FUTA tax (subtract line 3 from line 1).	4	
5	Minus: Total FUTA tax deposited for the year, including any overpayment applied from a prior year (from your records)	5	
6	**Balance due** (subtract line 5 from line 4). This should be $100 or less. Pay to IRS . . . . . . ▶	6	
7	**Overpayment** (subtract line 4 from line 5). Check if it is to be: ☐ Applied to next return, or ☐ Refunded . . ▶	7	

Part IV   Record of Quarterly Federal Tax Liability for Unemployment Tax (Do not include state liability.)

Quarter	First	Second	Third	Fourth	Total for Year
Liability for quarter					

Part V   Computation of Tentative Credit (Complete if you checked the "No" box in either question A or B or you checked the box in C, on page 1—see instructions.)

Name of state 1	State reporting number(s) as shown on employer's state contribution returns 2	Taxable payroll (as defined in state act) 3	State experience rate period 4		State experience rate 5	Contributions if rate had been 5.4% (col. 3 x .054) 6	Contributions payable at experience rate (col. 3 x col. 5) 7	Additional credit (col. 6 minus col.7) If 0 or less, enter 0. 8	Contributions actually paid to the state 9
			From—	To—					

10 Totals . . . . . ▶

11 Total tentative credit (add line 10, columns 8 and 9—see instructions for limitations) . . . . ▶

If you will not have to file returns in the future, write "Final" here (see general instruction "Who Must File") and sign the return. ▶

Under penalties of perjury, I declare that I have examined this return, including accompanying schedules and statements, and to the best of my knowledge and belief, it is true, correct, and complete, and that no part of any payment made to a state unemployment fund claimed as a credit was or is to be deducted from the payments to employees.

Signature ▶   Title (Owner, etc.) ▶   Date ▶

Form **940** (1988)

6

Obtaining Insurance

As with any business, child care centers need to consider the matter of insurance. Since child care is a service industry, special attention needs to be given to those types of insurance coverage needed by service businesses. Recently, the insurance industry has taken a new look at child care and the specific risks involved in providing child care for America's families. Although the "crisis" in child care insurance has eased somewhat, insurance issues will always remain an important concern.

Insurance policies and insurance is not an easy subject to understand. Careful review of policies, coverage, and premiums must always be done. There are professionals in the insurance industry with great expertise in their field who will assist you in determining your needs, evaluating coverage, and analyzing premiums. Don't hesitate to contact them, as well as the insurance commissioner's office within your state where valuable information can be garnered. Don't stop seeking information until all your questions are answered.

Liability Insurance

Although child care centers have a variety of insurance needs, the most critical is liability insurance. Liability insurance covers the operators of a child care facility if they are sued—whether it be due to neglect, injury, accident or allegation, and may also include coverage which addresses child abuse. After you have met your policy's deductible amount, a liability insurance policy covers the center for damages that might arise from a variety of claims.

In our litigious society, all responsible businesses must carry liability insurance. The fact that child care operators look after children for substantial periods of time increases their risk factors. The best way to protect yourself in these matters is to be adequately covered.

Property Insurance

Property insurance is another type of insurance that child care facilities should consider. This insurance covers the child care center in the event of property damage from fire, hail, wind, and other disasters. It may also cover theft, burglary, and vandalism. Since many child care facilities rent or lease, a clause in the lease agreement should designate who is responsible, the tenant or the landlord, for carrying property insurance. In some situations, the landlord may secure the insurance and then pass the cost along to the tenant. Determine whether it would be more cost effective to purchase it yourself.

Automobile or Vehicle Insurance

Another type of insurance to consider is vehicle insurance. If your center provides transportation services (i.e., transporting children from the center to school, from home to the center, or on area field trips), adequate insurance is a must. Although limitations of liability on coverage are set by each state, standard automobile/vehicle policies for a child care facility should cover personal property and liability in the event a center vehicle damages another person's vehicle or property. There are several caveats to automobile/vehicle insurance of which you should be aware. These include additional coverage for uninsured motorists, higher liability limits, coverage for drivers under age 25, drivers with poor driving records, and unowned vehicles. Unowned vehicle protection covers a center should a staff member, volunteer, or parent use their own vehicle in transacting center business.

Accidental Medical

Accidental medical insurance covers the "first dollars" of a claim resulting from accident. For example, if a child is injured on the playground of the child care facility, accidental medical insurance will cover the initial bills incurred as a result of the accident (i.e., doctor bills and emergency room bills). Customary limits of accidental medical insurance are $1,000 to $10,000 and can be purchased for a nominal fee. When a claim exceeds the coverage limits, the child care operator turns to his or her liability insurance policies.

Accidental medical has several advantages to the child care provider It allows a facility to take immediate action on a claim and to pay immediate medical bills. This can help alleviate tension between you and the family of a child that has been injured. It sets the family's mind at ease, assures them of your concern, and can divert potential lawsuits.

Association Policies

Several child care management and membership associations have developed group policies for the purchase of insurance by their members. The Child Care Center Associations of Arizona, Colorado, and Florida have put together package policy plans for their members at a reduced rate. In some cases, an association plan also involves a Self Insurance Retention fund (SIR). An SIR fund is created when a group partially insures the individual centers within their organization. When a claim is filed, the SIR pays an initial pre-determined deductible.

All states have an office of insurance or an insurance commissioner's office within their state government. The role of these offices is to license insurance companies to sell policies in the state and to act as a watch dog agency on behalf of the consumer.

Assessing Your Child Care Insurance Needs

- What is the physical size of your operation? How many children do you serve? (Many insurance companies charge a fee for liability insurance based on the number of children enrolled and assess a premium for property insurance based on the square footage in the facility.)

- Do you have a board of directors governing your organization? Does coverage extend to board members? What limit of liability coverage, if any, is acceptable to them?

- Are there state regulations dictating what types of insurance you must have? Do they define amounts of coverage?

- What are the areas of your operation you feel put you most at risk? Is it field trips, transportation services, or playgrounds? (It should be noted studies have shown playgrounds present the greatest risk to young children—80% to 90% of injuries to children in child care take place on the playground.)

- Have you solicited bids from several different insurance companies before purchasing your policies? Have you compared the premiums for group policies through your state associations with the premiums of independent agents?

- Do you clearly understand what your policies actually include? Since insurance policies only cover what is actually in writing, does the policy contain everything you have negotiated?

- Can you afford to purchase the insurance you will need? If you cannot pay the entire sum at one time, does your insurance company have payment plans?

Insurance can be one of your larger business expenses. Companies that do not have a payment plan may have a relationship with a company specializing in financing insurance coverage. In this case, you could enter into one agreement with the insurance company, and another with a finance company to arrange for payment to be made. Further, state associations often have established financing plans for their insurance programs.

7

Creating the Right Set-up

Location, Location, Location

It is often said the three most important considerations in starting a business are location, location, and location. The same holds true for child care services. A child care center built in a beautiful country setting without young families in the vicinity is doomed. Likewise, a child care center that is not accessible will not be used even if it is in an area surrounded by young children. Location is vital!

A child care operator recently opened a center next door to two brand new supermarkets. She chose the site feeling very confident the supermarkets must have done extensive demographic studies before selecting the location and deduced it must be a prime spot.

Although this may not be a scientific approach, demographic analysis is an important step in selecting a site. There are many sources of information for demographic studies. Nationally, the Bureau of Census has population data on all communities. Within your state, the department of human services may have information about child care facilities in the area. And don't overlook your local Welcome Wagon and Chamber of Commerce, which have some insight into the business climate in the area. Financial institutions, such as banks, are another possibility. Resource and Referral agencies may also have demographics about existing child care facilities and needs or gaps in child care services. Whatever the source might be, it is important to gather as much information as possible in order to make a well-informed decision.

Choosing a Site for Your Center

Q: What is the population you intend to serve?

Q: Where do they live?

Q: Is child care largely available in this area already? Is there a great demand for the service? Until recently, competition between child care programs was not an issue. Over the past ten years, however, the industry has grown and programs have proliferated. While it is possible for programs to work very well side-by-side, you will cut your chances for success if you overbuild in a particular area.

Q: Can people in this area afford to pay the fees you must charge?

Q: What kind of an early childhood program would this client population want? Is this program the kind you would like to offer?

Q: Are there pre-existing buildings in the area you have identified? Is there vacant land that can be built upon? Is there a church or synagogue that might consider housing a child care facility? What about other community buildings?

Q: Is the price of land within your budget?

Q: Is it zoned for child care centers? You must become familiar with zoning regulations in the area you have targeted. Many a good plan has hit a roadblock when it is discovered zoning codes do not allow child care facilities in the chosen area. Since zoning is determined locally, no clear-cut statements can be made about it. Each locality and defined areas within that locality are evaluated on a case-by-case basis. While some areas have very strict zoning regulations, other areas have none.

Q: Will the area surrounding the site grow and develop in the future? Will there be more families or less?

Q: What is the business climate in the area you have in mind? Are there employers in the vicinity who have substantial employee populations and are seeking child care?

CHOOSING A BUILDING

When and if you purchase or lease a building, there are several major points to consider. Before committing to any long-term arrangement for a building, be sure to have a professional conduct a thorough inspection of the structure and all of its major systems.

STRUCTURE

* Is the building well constructed? Is it made of sturdy material suited to the area's climate?

* Is the foundation sound? Are cracks or gaps visible?

* Has the ground settled, causing the building to shift? Are there cracks in the walls? Will the windows and doors open freely?

* Are there signs of inadequate drainage? Is the basement damp and musty smelling? Is there standing water anywhere in sight? Are there water stains visible on carpet or concrete?

* Does the roof appear to be in good shape? Are all the shingles in place? Are water stains visible on the walls and ceilings? Are the soffits and overhangs in good repair?

* Is the paint in good condition? Is it chipping or peeling?

* Are the walkways and steps in good repair? Will they handle the volume of foot traffic you are anticipating? Are the handrails safe and secure?

* Was asbestos used in the construction? Will removal be necessary?

* Has the radon level been checked? Is it within an acceptable range?

* Is there sufficient insulation for climate demands?

MECHANICAL SYSTEMS

The condition of the following major systems will be a critical factor in your decision to choose a building:
* Plumbing system
* Electrical system
* Heating system
* Ventilating system
* Air conditioning system
* Sprinkler system

Physical Set -Up

Although some people view the physical set- up of a center as an adventure—action-packed, fun-filled, and hands-on—others find it a tedious, time consuming, and money-gobbling chore. Whatever your perspective may be, the process is of critical importance. In many cases, the physical appearance of your center is what will—or won't—attract parents and children to take a closer look.

How you lay out your facility will be determined by several things:

- Every square foot must have a function and a purpose.

- All plans should be designed in accordance with state rules and regulations.

- Your physical plan must be reasonable, affordable, and have a long life expectancy.

- Furniture, fixtures, and equipment (FEE) must be purchased with respect to durability and practicality.

How to Choose Equipment

> Q: Is it safe (i.e., shatterproof, painted with nontoxic, lead-free paint, no small detachable parts for young children to swallow, free of splinters, points, and sharp edges)?
> Q: Is it easy to wash?
> Q: Is it durable? Will it stand up to children's hard use?
> Q: Will it interest kids for a sustained period of time?
> Q: Can it be used for more than one age group? Can youngsters grow up with it?
> Q: Can it be used creatively? Does it have more than one use?
> Q: Can it be used independently by a child or does it need adult supervision?
> Q: Can it be used cooperatively? Will it generate opportunities for group play?
> Q: Can it be used both indoors and outdoors?

Your Center's Appearance

EXTERIOR BUILDING APPEARANCE

If your facility is located within another community structure, such as a church or an office building, the changes you can make will be limited. If you own a free-standing building or have plans to purchase a property, you can usually make whatever alterations you choose.

When you design a physical plan for the exterior of your building, think about:

• What is the first impression people have when they see your building? It is imperative that both the first and lasting impression be positive. Parents will not enroll their children or have their kids continue to attend a program in a building about which they have concerns and reservations.

• Can you make it convenient for parents to drop-off and pick-up their children? Are there ample parking spaces? Is there easy access to the entrance of the center?

• Is the general landscaping appealing? Do you have a paved parking lot, trees, shrubs, or flower boxes? Even a traditional white picket fence can add to the exterior appeal of the center.

ENTRANCE WAYS

As prospective clients, enrolled families, and visitors arrive, the second impression they will have is the entry or front office area.

• Is your entry safe from a security standpoint? Would it be possible for a visitor to drift into the building? Could a child walk out of the center unattended without being seen?
An effort should be made to set up the entry so anyone entering or leaving the center must pass by some sort of checkpoint. Some child care facilities invest in elaborate systems for video taping all incoming and outgoing passages; others have a receptionist seated in the front office to monitor activity. Parents not only welcome these systems, they are beginning to demand them!

• Is it warm and cheerful? Are pieces of children's artwork displayed? Does it smell clean? Does it look well kept and orderly?

• Is someone readily available to greet newcomers?

• Is there a place where visitors or parents can sit down and feel at home?

- Is your entry or front office where parents sign-in and sign-out their children? If a center is small, this may be an ideal area. If the center has several rooms, it may be better to have check-in in each room to avoid a traffic jam. There are several options for the sign-in area. Some centers choose to place an attractive desk or table in a prominent area with the appropriate sign-in sheet on top. Others have sign-in counters which are appealing looking and space efficient.

CLASSROOMS

Children who are in full-day care may spend 10 or 11 hours a day in the classroom and on the playground. Parents who are seeking child care will look for a classroom that appears warm and inviting—a place where their children would feel comfortable spending extended periods of time.

- Does the room look clean? Does there seem to be some organization to it or is it cluttered? Is it very crowded?
  Although early childhood classrooms are busy places, they don't always have to look like disaster struck. Children are learning to clean up after themselves, and teachers model these habits.

- Are pieces of children's artwork hung on the walls? Are they low enough so children can see them? Are there other bright posters on the walls?

- Is equipment on low open shelves so it is accessible to children? Is there a good choice of materials?

- Is there a place for youngsters to put their belongings when they come to school? Cubbies? Shelves?

- Is there space designated as quiet space? Places where children can go when they need some privacy?

- Is the classroom designed so that caregivers can see all of the children?

- Is it painted and carpeted in soft colors that suggest a relaxed and calming atmosphere?

PLAYGROUND

Knowing that play is the primary occupation of young children, development of your center's playground becomes a crucial component in your setup. Many child care providers think the larger the playground, the better. However, the design and types of equipment available are much more important than sheer space. For basic playground design refer to Diagram 6.1.

Technically, the rules and regulations of your state may call for two different types of surfaces on your playground; paved or hard surfaces and a soft, grassy area. The standard paved area, be it cement or blacktop, facilitates group games, riding toys, and other large motor activity. Other options include a new rubber-type surface with interlocking pieces. As this is a fairly new concept, do careful research on durability and cost.

Wood chips and tree bark are not recommended for playground use under any circumstances. Wood chips splinter, footing is poor, and they may not offer a good subsurface for drainage and continual play. If you include a gravel area in your playground design, pea gravel is ideal. The small, washed stone offers fairly secure footing and good drainage. Injuries seem to be somewhat less severe in an area that has pea gravel versus a paved surface.

A shady, grassy area is an ideal place for picnic lunches, storytelling, group games, and just plain frolicking. If your playground is limited in size, however, grassy areas can be difficult to maintain with the constant wear of little feet.

Regardless of what surfaces you include in your design, sand—be it in a boxed area or a large sunken open space—is a must. Despite the fact that many parents complain they have half the sandbox in their kitchen when their children return home at the end of the day, it is important to keep the sandbox continually filled.

To keep up with the developing child, playgrounds must be designed to foster the physical, cognitive, emotional, and social growth of the young child. Superstructures might include swings, bridges, slides, and climbers. Natural elements, such as sand and water, should be readily available. Tools of play, including shovels, buckets, balls, jump ropes, and riding toys should be accessible at any time. The playground environment must have plenty of open space with superstructures allowing areas for dramatic play and other imaginative activities.

All space, including those fun "hideaways," should be visible for easy staff observation.

Remembering to design your playground to reflect the developmental needs of children will add a depth to your program that will encourage the growth and development of its young occupants to their fullest potential.

Furniture, Fixtures, and Equipment
Infant Care

Adequate space is required for furniture, fixtures, and equipment needed to care for infants. When designing a room for infants, carefully consider how feeding, changing, playing, and sleeping routines impact your plan. For basic infant care floor plan refer to Diagram 6.2.

• Plans should include adequate plumbing facilities to allow for one or more sinks within the classroom. A hand-washing sink should be adjacent to all diaper changing facilities. If any food preparation is done in the infant area, such as the mixing of formula, a separate sink should be placed for that purpose.

• A diaper changing area should be accessible and centrally located so teachers can still see the other infants in their care. The changing area should have a smooth, washable surface and adequate storage space so diaper supplies can be reached without the caregiver leaving the diapering area. A sanitary system for the disposal of diapers must be implemented.

• Provision must be made for storage and display of equipment. The use of low shelves, open cabinets, and functional table-top storage are options.

• Infant seats have become popular. "Sassy seats" which attach to table tops in a secure manner and tables with seat cutouts with plastic inserts are commonly used for infants of an appropriate age.

• Holding a baby closely is still an essential part of the bonding process, so adequate provision must be made for the caregivers to hold the infants repeatedly and for extended periods during the day. The opportunity for holding an infant during feeding must be given top priority. Keeping this in mind, it is important to provide the caregiver with comfortable seating arrangements, such as rocking chairs that are conducive to holding infants.

• Sufficient space for walking with an infant should be built into the classroom design.

• Washable surfaces on walls and floors are favored. Since most infants are not yet walking, softer cushioning floor materials in certain areas of the room should be used.

• An unbreakable, shatterproof, low-level mirror is a nice addition in an infant room. The mirror must be securely attached.

• Adequate sleeping facilities, such as playpens and/or cribs, need to be provided and arranged so infants may have waking and resting periods according to their own schedules. This may mean placing some of the sleeping facilities in a secluded area in the room to minimize the potential for disturbance, yet offer adequate supervision.

• Other miscellaneous items to consider when designing and equipping an infant room include: a small refrigerator for proper storage of infant formula and food; a food warmer, microwave oven, or bottle warmer for heating infant food or formula/milk; and an adequate supply of drinking water for mixing formula or food.

Equipment List for Infant Room

Rattles, soft toys, stuffed animals, hard books (plastic, plastic coated, or fabric), drums for banging, grip balls, mobiles, teething rings, squeaky toys, balls of all sizes, soft blocks, push toys, ankle-wrist bracelets, activity boxes or busy boxes, containers for putting things in and taking them out, peg boards with large pegs, pictures for walls, and a shatterproof mirror. Also, high chairs, refrigerator, warming tray or microwave, diaper pail, record player, blankets, sheets, infant seats, cribs, play pens, changing table, and infant swing.

Toddler Programs

The furniture, fixtures, equipment, and room design for toddler care resembles in many ways the infant room, but differences do exist. These should accommodate toddlers' increased mobility, changing dietary requirements, and toilet habits. A primary concern in the design of a classroom for toddler care should be safety. For basic toddler care floor plan refer to Diagram 6.3.

• Many toddlers are just learning to walk and are quite unsteady on their feet, so surfaces must be chosen that are easy to maneuver on. Adequate open space should be available so toddlers can practice the art of moving around on their feet. Often, toddler programs have built-in steps, ramps, and platforms for toddlers to play on.

• Toddlers still have a need for close contact with adults. To facilitate this contact, low comfortable chairs, rocking chairs, and soft comfortable surfaces on the floor for sitting all add to the warmth of the room.

- In addition, these tykes do extensive climbing. A small climbing apparatus will assist them in the development of this skill.

- The need for more equipment—such as balls, toys, and games—increases and so too does the need for more extensive open shelf storage and display. Toddlers must have equipment accessible to them at all times. Classrooms are often divided into several activity centers including dramatic play, art, small motor, and large motor.

- Younger toddlers still are in diapers and will need proper changing facilities. A changing table or counter should have a smooth, washable surface or disposable single-use coverings. Storage for diapering supplies should be accessible to the caregiver and adequate in space to house the diapers.

- A hand-washing sink in the immediate vicinity of the changing area is also recommended. Studies have shown that proper hand-washing techniques by caregivers can reduce the incidents of communicable diseases significantly. Do not simply have hand-washing facilities available, but be sure to make them readily accessible and convenient to use. Sinks for children should be located near toilets so youngsters can easily wash their hands after each toilet experience.

- As toddlers begin to learn to use the toilet, adequate bathroom facilities are needed. A partially separated bathroom area with easy access by children is recommended. Many toddlers enjoy having company to visit with while spending short intervals of time in or near the toilet facility.

This can be accomplished through the installation of child-size toilets in close proximity. Larger toddler programs may even choose to install more than two toilets.

Toilet facilities in a toddler program should be as open to view as possible. Since toilet training activities can sometimes be viewed as an opportunity for abuse or improper handling of a situation, the more open to view the toilet facility is, the lower the risk involved can be.

Other important considerations in the set-up of the toddler environment include:

- An adequate supply of drinking water is available to a toddler at all times during the day. This may mean some type of drinking fountain or installation of a disposable cup dispenser.

- Access to an appropriately equipped playground area is a must for these youngsters.

- Smooth, cleanable floor surfaces in eating areas are recommended. Even the simplest and neatest snack suddenly becomes the source for a mess when placed in the hands of a young child.

- Adequate rest surfaces—such as mats, cots, or cribs—need to be included in the planned toddler classroom. Similar to infants, toddlers may need rest periods according to their own individual schedules. The design of the toddler activity area should be such that quiet, peaceful areas are available for toddlers to rest in without disturbing others in the group. Of course they should remain under the constant supervision of their caregiver.

- Toddlers, especially younger ones may require bottle feeding. Equipment necessary for the storage of their food may still be necessary. In larger programs that employ cooks or staff members specifically for food preparation, this task may be assigned to that person.

Equipment for Toddlers

Some infant equipment will continue to be appropriate for toddlers. Additional equipment often includes: jack in the box, flash-lights, dolls, plastic figures, sorting games, simple puzzles, stacking toys, rocking horse, fat crayons, paper, nesting toys lids and bottles, push and pull toys, pounding bench, doll strollers, dress-up clothes, musical instruments, housekeeping tools, digging tools, carpentry tools, blankets and sheets for tents, riding toys, soft and wooden blocks, child-sized tables and chairs, water table, dramatic play fixtures, adequate shelving, and record player.

Preschool Care

Preschool children need a large space in which to move around. Three and four-year-old children need to move about freely without feeling crowded or cramped. In many of their activity projects, group games, and scheduled routines will require space and the ability to spread out. Preschool classrooms are generally divided into activity centers: art, small motor, math or writing, dramatic play, science, sensory area, lock area, carpentry, music, and reading.

Following are commonly identified "activity centers" for the preschool child and some ideas for equipment and materials. These will vary by the age group of children in the classroom. Youngsters should be allowed to move equipment and materials from one center to another. No matter what the age, however, centers should always be well stocked and materials should be readily accessible to young children. For basic preschool floor plan refer to Diagram 6.4.

Art Center Materials

PAPER: Assorted colors and sizes of butcher block, construction paper, finger paint, newspaper, computer paper, lined, paper towel, carbon, tissue, cellophane, wall paper samples, tinfoil.

PAINT: Assorted colors of finger paints, tempera, watercolors.

BRUSHES: Large and small brushes, cotton swabs, feathers, toothpicks, empty deodorant applicators, sticks, toothbrushes.

Magic Markers, crayons, colored pencils, pens and pencils, chalk, juice jars, toilet paper and paper towel rolls, straws, beans, cotton balls, ribbons, twigs, leaves, sponges for printing, old magazines, cards, pipe cleaners, glitter, stickers, glue, paste, Scotch Tape, masking tape, rubber bands, paper punch, eye droppers, scissors, ink pads, ink stamps, rulers, Playdough, Silly Putty, modeling clay.

Small Motor

The small motor area may include a math and writing center (these are separated in many classrooms). Cuisinaire rods, board games, letter/number blocks, calculators, adding machines, puzzles, Legos, locking blocks, nesting toys, old machines to take apart, dominoes, peg boards, card games, parquetry blocks, nuts and bolts, magnetic letters, numbers, Etch-a-Sketch, bristle blocks, buttons, beads for stringing, Tinker Toys, snap/tie/zip toys, typewriter, pens, paper, scissors, construction toys, lotto games, sewing cards.

Sensory Area
WATER TABLE:

Every preschool classroom must have a water table. If you use water in it, there are many variations: water with bubbles, cold and warm, ice cubes, soap, food coloring, extracts (peppermint, lemon, banana), snow, dirt, or cornstarch.

Accessories for water play include measuring cups, small pans, pitchers, coffee cups, funnels, clear plastic tubing, corks to fill the ends of the tubes, marbles for inside the tubes, egg beater, wooden spoons, plastic squeeze bottles, colanders, sponges (natural, synthetic, thick, thin, various colors), washcloths, paint brushes, floor mop, baster, medicine droppers, ice cube trays, syringes, water wheels, and pump bottle. You can also use other imaginative things such as sand, mud, rice, beans, cornmeal, oatmeal, styrofoam packing squiggles, and other styrofoam shapes,

BUBBLES:

A good mixture for bubbles is 3/4 cup liquid soap, 1/4 cup glycerine, and 2 quarts water.

Accessories for bubble blowing include funnels, paper tubes, styrofoam cups with a straw stuck in the side, straws, wire loops, plastic six-pack holders, strawberry baskets, and bubble frames.

SAND PLAY:

Any kind of sand is good, but silica sand (very fine and white) is especially fun.

Accessories for sand play include spoons, scoops, shovels, cans, bottles, buckets, funnels, sand wheels, colanders, sifters of varying gauges, various grades of woven cloth, cars, trucks, plastic figures, siphon tubes, buckets for water, and sand combs.

Block Area

BLOCKS: wooden unit, large plastic, small Legos, snap blocks, cardboard, bristle blocks, soft blocks.

OTHER: Train and track set, cars, planes, trucks, signs, boats, plastic or wooden figures, long wooden slats, balls (small and large), wagon.

Dramatic Play

FOR HOUSEKEEPING: stove, refrigerator, sink, play food, doll bed, doll high chair, chairs and table, cupboard, stroller for dolls, cash register, dolls, dress-up clothes, dishes, foods, blankets, pillows, shopping carts, puppets, doll house with furniture and people, telephone, iron, housecleaning tools (broom, duster, vacuum).

DRAMATIC PLAY KITS:

Service station/car wash: caps, overalls, rags, hoses, tools, squeegee, buckets, sponges.

Monster Box: old sheets, masks, costumes, makeup, plastic nails, nose, fangs.

Circus Box: makeup, ruffled collars, cone hat, funny glasses, baggy pants, old ties.

Beauty or Barber Shop: mirrors, brushes and combs, makeup, cologne, empty razors, rollers, manicure utensils, hair dryer, washcloth, colored hair mousse.

Camping Trip: fishing poles, small tent, old backpacks, camping dishes, cook stove, old sleeping bag, compass, flashlight.

Hospital: stethoscope, strips of sheets for Band-Aids, crutches, pajamas, empty syringes, Band-Aids, blood pressure gauge, tongue depressors, pads/pens, scrubs, nurses hat, cotton balls, clip board/chart.

Fire Station: hoses, boots, truck, pants, ladder, alarm clock, fire extinguisher, hats.

Travel Bureau: travel posters, brochures, tickets, envelopes, forms, suitcases, miniature airplanes, buses, trains, ships, airline baggage.

Reading Area

BOOKS: Big, small, hard, soft, pictures only, word books. Also a mattress, soft pillows, blankets, soft lighting, soft music, plants, aquarium, shelves to display books, stuffed animals, story tapes, and cassette player.

Music Area

EQUIPMENT: cassette recorder, tapes, record player, records, tambourines, kazoos, wooden sand blocks, head sets, rhythm sticks, drums, cymbals, bells, piano or organ, microphone, xylophone.

Carpentry Area

Workbench, vise, saw, hammer, screw driver, nails, glue, wood scraps, bottle caps.

Science Area

Nature posters, bird eggs, nests, pine cones, shells, ant farm, butterfly collection, magnifying glasses, flashlight, rocks, science books, magnets, scale, microscope, tree bark, terrarium.

Equipment for the School-Aged Child

Many-pieced puzzles, kites, sports equipment, collections (stamps, comic books, rocks), board games, card games, sewing/weaving, extensive construction tools and workbench, guitars, ukeleles, Autoharps, recorders, jump ropes, Frisbees, bicycles, roller skates/ ice skates, magazines, typewriter or computer, number and letter games.

Playground Diagram 6.1

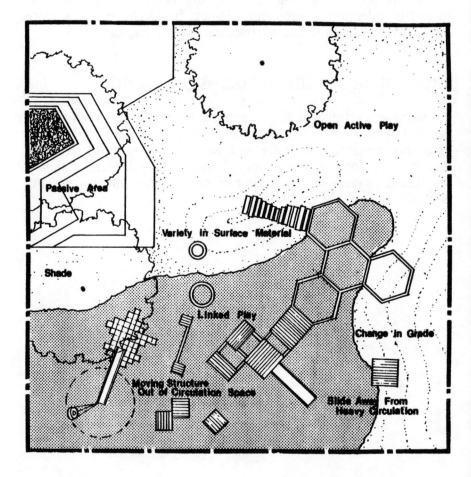

Infant Floor Plan
Diagram 6.2

EXAMPLE:

AREA: 500 s.f. ea. (2 rooms)
        50 s.f. infant
        10 infants max./room

SPACE:

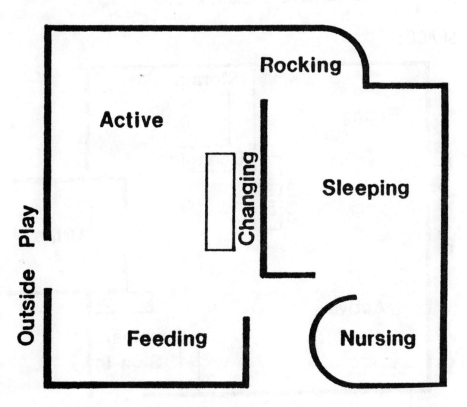

Toddler Floor Plan
Diagram 6.3

EXAMPLE:

AREA: 675 s.f. each (4 rooms)
       45 s.f./toddler if combined sleeping
       & play
       30 s.f./toddler if sleeping & play
       is separated
       15 toddlers max./room

SPACE:

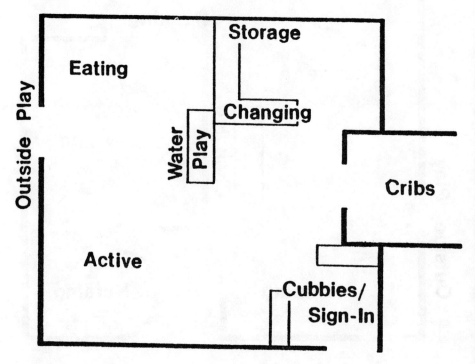

Preschool Floor Plan
Diagram 6.4

EXAMPLE:

AREA: 900 s.f. ea. (3 rooms)
        30 s.f./child
        30 children max./room

SPACE:

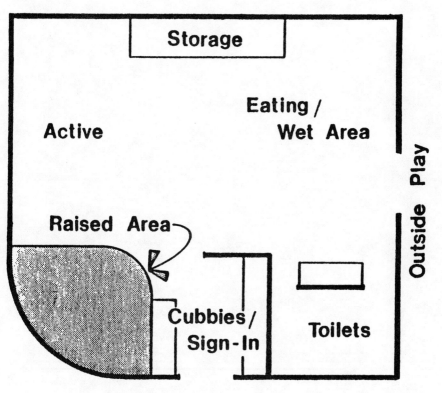

8

Marketing Your Program

"There was an old woman,
Who lived in a shoe,
She had so many children,
She didn't know what to do!"

Most child care centers attempting to get their businesses off the ground or to maintain a comfortable level of business activity would give anything to be like the old woman in the shoe. For caregivers, this is however, an ideal circumstance. The reality of the matter is securing and maintaining a satisfactory number of enrollments is crucial. To accomplish this, a marketing plan must be designed and implemented.

The marketing plan you institute should have two components: identifying individual, personal factors that make you unique and implementing general marketing concepts and techniques.

Your Unique Approach

You need to analyze carefully what your competitors, those other child care centers in your general vicinity, are offering families. Survey their approach to the business of child care, their program, their staff, and their curriculum. With that information in hand, you then need to analyze how your program is different and what factors set you apart from the rest. Now capitalize on those differences!

There are many advertising and publicity techniques you can employ to attract parents and children to your doors. It is the personal attention you give families once they walk in that will cause them to enroll and stay at your child care center. Always remember what people think you are—their perception—is their reality.

Marketing Techniques

Advertising and publicizing your child care center to recruit clients is a key factor in your marketing plan. Advertising comes in many forms and has a variety of price tags attached.

WORD OF MOUTH:

Business experts tell us that "word of mouth" is the very best way to advertise. Word of mouth advertising occurs when a parent of a child who is currently enrolled in your program or has been enrolled in your program in the recent past tells another parent about you. Since parents often view other parents as excellent judges of the quality of your services, program and staff, a good word from a satisfied customer goes a long way in convincing a perspective parent that your facility may meet their needs as well.

One center in the Chicago area actually rewarded parents for spreading the good word about their center. Families received "reimbursement" vouchers for every successful referral made to another family. The voucher was credited toward their child care bill. This system proved a great success. Another child care center in Flagstaff, Arizona, posted all notes and letters of appreciation received from families they had served on a parent bulletin board. They were sure to point this out to prospective clients as they toured the facility.

Solicited comments from parents can also be reprinted in the child care center's promotional literature to convey the positive attitude other parents have about that facility. Word-of-mouth advertising can take some time to develop, but if you do a good job providing the needed services and satisfying your families, they will assist you in spreading the good word about your center.

SIGNS

Signage is a direct way of communicating to the general public your center's name, the types of services you offer, and other important information about your facility. A well-placed, attractive sign is often the single most effective way to advertise your center. "Bright," "colorful," and "easy to read" are the buzz words in designing a sign. If vehicular traffic is your target audience, be sure all lettering can be read from a distance. Cars traveling by have only a few seconds to read the message you place on your sign. Select that message carefully.

When lighting is available for your sign, it can add dramatically to effectiveness and readability. Lighting specific highlights of a sign allows for continued reading in hours of darkness. Many local communities have introduced very specific sign codes. Be sure you are aware of these codes.

DIRECTORY ADVERTISING

Display ads and in-column listings in your local telephone directories, child care directories, and the advertising booklets can be very important in getting the word out about your center. Newcomers to your area, parents who are making changes in their child care arrangements, and old-fashioned curiosity seekers may look to these directories for information about child care services. Careful consultation with an advertising directory representative will allow you to design the type of ad you would like at a price you can afford. Since directory advertising is costly, but cost effective, consider all the factors before making a decision.

FLYERS AND BROCHURES

Many centers have experienced great success in increasing enrollment with the use of fliers and brochures. Printed materials about your child care center should include all the necessary pieces of information parents need to understand the service you offer. The name of your center, address, and telephone number should be prominent. Other information, such as hours of operation, services offered, and special features need to be highlighted as well. Parents should feel welcome to visit your center after reading a flier or brochure. For many parents, a printed pamphlet will often be the first impression they have of your center. Make that impression a good one. Cheerful photos, crisp designs, and catchy graphics are all well used here.

PUBLICITY

Publicizing your child care center is of equal importance to boosting enrollment. Publicity can be defined as advertising that is free of charge. You, as the operator of a child care facility, can create opportunities for publicity. Prior to the actual opening of a center, the construction, renovation, or equipping of your child care center is often newsworthy in community publications and local newspapers.

Keep in mind when seeking publicity, if photos are to be used, they must be black and white. Local community publications often desire short stories with photos of "happenings" in the community. The establishment of a new child care facility is of interest to a great many readers.

Likewise, a grand opening event is worthy of publication. Depending on the level of news activity in your area, radio and television stations may be interested in interviewing someone from the new child care center in the community. There are a myriad of events you can plan and schedule to foster public attention. For example: news conferences by local political figures can be scheduled to occur at your facility. Carnivals, parades, and celebrations often make their way onto the pages of your local press. This is an area where creativity and imagination, as well as a little boldness, can reap major benefits in getting the word out about your center. And all of this for free!

Resource and Referral Agencies

Child Care Resource and Referral agencies are developing in local communities across the country at a rapid rate. Resource and Referral agencies are often the magic link between available child care services and families in need of care. Call your local Resource and Referral agency to be sure you are listed and eligible to receive child care referrals.

9

Working with Employers

Recognizing the impact projected workforce demographics will have on a company's ability to do business, we have seen a dramatic increase in corporate sector involvement in the issues of child care.

Options for employers run the gambit from "cafeteria" benefit plans to enhanced resource and referral services. While only 4,000 of the country's six million businesses offer some type of child care related benefit, is it represents a tremendous increase in the past decade. This trend opens new opportunities for child care providers offering direct services.

On-Site and Near-Site Child Care Centers

On-site child care is the most visible option an employer can offer. According to Dana Friedman of the Families and Work Institute in New York, about 150 companies and 400 hospitals have created child care centers for their employees. Some well-known employer sponsored on-site programs can be found at Stride Rite, Wang Laboratories, and Hoffman-Larouche.

Since most companies are in businesses other than child care, corporations often look to third party providers to supply child care services for them.

• Corning Glass Works and Merck Pharmaceutical provided the start-up funds for private nonprofit centers which rely on user fees for operating expenses.

• The city of Denver's new convention center is one of the first in the country to offer on-site child care for conventioneers' children. Operated by a third party provider, an RFP process (Request for Proposal of third-party providers) was used to select this provider.

• Cigna Corporation and Campbell Soup contract with Kinder-Care to run their on-site program.

Vendor Programs

Another popular option for employers is a vendor program where the employer arranges for the purchase of a designated number of spaces to be reserved for company employees in an existing child care center nearby. This can be more appealing to companies if some kind of discount for employee children can be negotiated (5% to 10%).

Contributions

Other companies choose to become involved with child care by adopting a child care center and offering in-kind services, donations of goods and equipment, or volunteers for a special project.

As the network of child care Resources and Referral agencies continues to grow across the U.S., most employers are turning to them for technical assistance regarding employer supported child care benefits. If working with corporations is an avenue you wish to explore, a good first step is to contact your local Resource and Referral agency. They can provide information on what is happening with the corporate sector in your community and how you can get involved.

10

Hiring Qualified Staff

The quality of your child care program will depend to a large extent on the quality of the staff you hire. It will be well worth the amount of time and effort you spend in the recruiting and hiring process to find the right employees. This process will require you to:

- Define your staffing needs.
- Determine what salary and benefits you can offer.
- Develop job descriptions detailing position responsibilities.
- Actively recruit and solicit applications.
- Interview candidates.
- Narrow down the pool of applicants.
- Screen and select staff.

Define Your Staffing Needs

State rules and regulation guidelines dictate staff/child ratios. Determine the number of teachers you need in accordance with the number of children you will serve. This includes aide positions as well. You may choose to hire more staff than is required by the state. In addition, consider whether or not you need a cook and/or assistant for food preparation, janitorial staff, drivers, an assistant director, administrative support staff, and others.

Determine Salary and Benefits

You can determine from your projected budget what your personnel costs will be. The largest expense you have will be personnel costs. It is estimated that 50% to 90% of a total child care budget is used to pay staff.

Develop Position Descriptions

Outline what it is you want your staff to be responsible for doing on the job.

POSITION DESCRIPTION: DIRECTOR

The director of the XYZ Center is responsible to the center owner for the administration of the center. Included within these responsibilities are the following:

1. Administration of the child care program in accordance with state rules and regulations.
2. Overall management of staff and delegation of work; interviewing, hiring, and orienting new staff members.
3. Completion of formal evaluations of staff.
4. Coordinates on-going staff training.
5. Maintains a child care program that meets the emotional, physical, intellectual, and social needs of the individual child and group. Supervises the implementation of the program.
6. Conducts informal and formal center evaluations.
7. Maintains open communications with parents to ensure good continuing relationships.
8. Serves in a leadership role as it relates to both management and instructional programming.
9. Responsible for overall fiscal management of the center.
10. Assumes responsibility for the day-to-day operation of the center.

POSITION DESCRIPTION: ASSISTANT DIRECTOR

The assistant director of the child care center is responsible to the director of the center and serves as acting director in his/her absence.
1. Works with the director and other staff in a team approach to develop a high quality educational child care program.

2. Assists the director in administering the child care center in accordance with state rules and regulations.
3. Assists the director in the overall organization and delegation of work.
4. Administers the food service program and USDA record keeping; is responsible for menu planning.
5. Works with teachers to establish material and equipment needs and priorities to meet program needs. Coordinates the distribution of supplies, curriculum materials, and equipment.
6. Develops center staffing pattern to meet program standards.
7. Assists director in developing a budget for the center.
8. Supervises aides and administrative staff.

POSITION DESCRIPTION: SUPERVISING TEACHER/CAREGIVER

Supervising teachers:

1. Manage the classroom program.
2. Supervise and guides each child's development.
3. Plan and organize classroom curriculum.
4. Coordinate the classroom teaching team.
5. Provide feedback to the members of the team.
6. Maintain appropriate records.
7. Work with parents.
8. Participate in center events.
9. Assist in the training of other staff members.
10. Additional duties as assigned.

POSITION DESCRIPTION: ASSISTING TEACHER/CAREGIVER

Assisting teachers are responsible for:

1. Assisting supervising teacher in carrying out the entire classroom program.
2. Assisting in the supervision and guidance of the child's development. Maintains a positive, safe, and healthy classroom environment.
3. Assisting in the planning and organizing of classroom activities as assigned by the supervising teacher.

4. Participating in the classroom teaching team by working cooperatively with all team members.
5. Assisting in the maintenance of appropriate records as assigned by supervising teacher.
6. Working with parents under the direction of supervising teacher.
7. Acting as supervising teacher in his/her absence.
8. Participating in center events.
9. Additional duties as assigned.

POSITION DESCRIPTION: TEACHER AIDE

Teacher aides will:

1. Supervise activities in area(s) assigned by supervising or assisting teachers.
2. Assist in maintaining a neat, clean classroom.
3. Assist classroom teaching staff in implementing early childhood program.

Actively Recruit Staff

In order to draw from the widest pool of candidates, you may want to use several recruitment techniques:

CLASSIFIED ADVERTISEMENTS

Advertising for staff in your area's large daily or small community publications is a good place to start your recruitment campaign. Many of the large dailies recommend you place ads in the Sunday paper because distribution is higher and people typically have more leisure time to browse through the classified section on Sunday.

If you need to staff your entire center, you may choose to place a "general hiring" notice:

EXAMPLE:

New child care center seeks well trained, experienced staff to fill the positions of assistant director, teacher, aide, and cook. Center offers competitive salary and benefits for some positions, reduced child care costs, and training opportunities. Send resume to Jane Doe, XYZ Child Care Center, 123 Main Street, Anytown, USA 12345.

Depending on your advertising budget and particular needs, you may place separate ads for each position. This gives you the freedom to be more specific about job requirements. Advertisements can be quite extensive and formal as in this example:

The XYZ Center is accepting applications for the position of director. The center provides year round, high quality child care for 175 children age one to eight years. The staff includes 10 full-time professionals, plus additional part-time support staff.

Responsibilities include the development of an exemplary educational program; administration and financial management of center with annual budget of $ <u>000</u> ; supervision, training, and evaluation of staff; and liaison with parents and other community agencies.

Qualifications:Three years' experience teaching in an early childhood classroom; a minimum of three years' administrative experience. Computer experience preferred. Bachelor's degree in early childhood education, child development, or a related field required.

Salary: Commensurate with experience.

Application: Submit a letter of application, resume, and names, addresses, and phone numbers of reference to: Jane Doe, XYZ Child Care Center

123 Main Street, Anytown, U.S.A. 12345.

Position descriptions are available upon request.

Deadline for application is June 17, 1999, at 5:00 P.M.

Or...less detailed:

Director needed for new child care center. Full-time competitive salary and benefit package available for the right person. Position requires early childhood related college degree and minimum of three years' administrative and/or child care experience. Computer experience preferred. Only those with a commitment to quality child care need apply. Send resume to Jane Doe, XYZ Child Care, 123 Main Street, Anytown, U.S.A. 12345. Position description available upon request.

JOB ANNOUNCEMENTS

Another effective way to find qualified staff is to prepare a job announcement which can be sent to many different sources. A job announcement should include a description and mission statement of the child care center itself, a description of the position, a list of qualifications, salary information, application requirements, address, a deadline, and will look like the extensive advertisement for the director.

To be effective, you will want to distribute your announcement using many logical sources. Ask each source to post the notices on bulletin boards and/or publish the information in appropriate newsletters. Sources might include:

- College early childhood education training programs.
- Local Resource and Referral agencies.
- Local child care center support groups.
- Early childhood professional groups (i.e., NAEYC affiliates and Family Child Care Associations).
- High school home economics programs.
- Licensed child care centers in the state.
- Neighborhood churches.
- Local job service hot lines.
- State employment offices.
- Local school parent/teacher groups.

WORD OF MOUTH

Do not underestimate the value of word-of-mouth communication in the recruitment process. Tell everyone you know about the jobs you have available. Ask them to tell their friends!

Interview Candidates

The interview process will help you narrow down potential candidates. You may wish to include other people in the interview: a parent, your assistant director, or a teacher. Write down your questions beforehand and ask all of the candidates the same basic questions so they have equal opportunity to address the important issues you have identified.

Sample questions might be:

GENERAL BACKGROUND:

- Tell me about yourself. Why are you interested in this position?
- What kind of experience have you had working with children? Have you had any experience in a center setting? If yes, please describe.
- What is your educational background? Are you director/teacher qualified?

- Where do you see yourself professionally in the next five years?
- What are your strengths? What are your weaknesses?

FOR TEACHERS:

- Please describe your *ideal* classroom. How would the room be organized and arranged? What do visitors see when they walk into your room?
- Describe your approach to discipline.
- How would you involve children in making decisions about their learning?
- How would you encourage social interaction in your classroom?
- What educational goals do you have for children?
- Have you had any background in parent involvement or parent education programs? What is the role of the parent in a child care program?

FOR DIRECTORS:

- Please relate information about your administrative experience.
- Describe your *ideal* child care center. What methods would you use to help this center match that ideal?
- What is your philosophy on early childhood education?
- How would you encourage professional development among your staff?
- How would you handle a parent who always seems to be disgruntled about some aspect of the center's services?
- How would you formally and informally evaluate your program?
- What is a high quality child care program?

Narrow Down the Pool

Prior to selecting the final candidates, you should personally check their references. A quick call to former employers, especially in the child care field, colleagues, and other listed references will give you valuable insight into the capabilities and work habits of the people you are considering. Be sure to ask if the person is eligible for re-hire. This will give a good indication of any troublesome areas in their employment history. You might also ask the references if they are aware of any circumstances that might interfere with this applicant's ability to work effectively with young children. References are often reluctant to share negative information with callers; listen with more than your ears!

Select and Screen

Careful consideration of the prospects will lead to your final selection. Following are some criteria for selecting staff:

* Can you work compatibly with this person?
* Will this person fit in with your team?
* Does this person blend well with your overall program goals and objectives?

More detailed employment screening techniques, such as criminal record checks, child abuse registry checks, and motor vehicle record checks are being implemented by a number of child care centers across the country. Some states may actually call for one or more of these checks in the rules and regulations for child care. Review your state's rules to determine their specific requirements.

What to Look for In a Caregiver

[ ] Caregiver is sensitive to children's needs.
[ ] Caregiver has warmth, compassion, and a sense of humor.
[ ] Caregiver is knowledgeable about the development of children.
[ ] Caregiver is in good physical and mental health.
[ ] Caregiver has good references.
[ ] Caregiver is energetic and positive.
[ ] Caregiver has an open and comfortable communication style.
[ ] Caregiver shares your early childhood education philosophy.

Staff Notes

Staff Notes

11

Working with Parents

Both research and common sense tell us that parents, as children's primary caregivers, are the most important influence on their youngster's life. As such, no child care program can overlook the valuable input parents can offer—both about their children and about their own needs and desires relating to parenting and child care. When parents are actively involved in their children's early education, they feel better about using child care. Additionally, the center reaps the benefits of their strong support, enrollment remains high, and children are more likely to have a successful experience.

For many owners and directors of child care centers, dealing with parents can be one of the most stressful and demanding tasks of the job. Child care personnel ask, "What do I do with the parent who always complains?" or "How do I handle the parent who never pays their bill on time?" Others wonder how they can involve parents in program activities such as fund-raising or as volunteers in the classroom.

A major hurdle for many child care administrators is understanding parents. Too often, center administrators set themselves up for problems by assuming the role of an all-knowing expert on children. Striving for a mutually supportive partnership between parents and center staff is ideal.

Assess your own feelings and beliefs about a parent's role in a child care program.

- Do you believe the relationship between a parent and a child is the most important one?

- Do you believe most parents want the best for their children; that even when they do things that lead you to believe otherwise, they have the good of their child in mind?
- Do you believe parental involvement can enhance the quality of your program?
- Do you believe parents are the experts when it comes to their child?

Getting Parents Involved

There are several things you can do to facilitate parents' involvement and investment in your program. It is important you keep in mind the nature of the clientele you serve when you plan support services for parents.

DEVELOPING A PARENT HANDBOOK is a good way to welcome new parents into your school and give them important information they need to know.

Handbooks can be distributed to parents during their initial orientation meeting or when their children start in the program. The handbook can be designed formally or informally. It should cover general information (billing information, staff, parental involvement opportunities, meals, classroom policies); center policies (hours of operation, forms, fees); educational philosophy; and health policies (medical records, sick child care, medication, medical conditions, contagious disease).

NEW PARENT ORIENTATION SESSIONS can help to get you both off to a great start. They typically run a half hour to an hour. Set aside adequate time and keep interruptions to a minimum so you communicate how important this family is to your center. When you are available to answer questions, review policies, and get to know new parents, you prevent a great deal of miscommunication and potential alienation. Orientations are a good time to focus on the importance of parent participation and to review the opportunities for parent involvement.

GET ACQUAINTED NIGHT is often held at the beginning of the year. It is designed to provide parents with the opportunity to meet classroom teachers, administrators, and other parents in order to help them find out more about their child's experiences. Teachers can share information on activities, policies, educational goals and objectives. Parental concerns and questions should also be addressed. Refreshments are often a pleasant complement. Children can either attend with their parents or child care could be offered in another room. Consider initiating some type of ice breaker activity to help everyone relax.

PARENT CONFERENCES are often scheduled on a yearly or bi-yearly basis. Teachers need to be prepared for the conference and view it as part of their professional role as an early childhood educator. Conferences are a time when teachers can share information with parents on how their child is doing. Parents should have plenty of time to ask questions and share any information on specific issues, such as home life, or behavior that can help teachers better understand the child. The teacher should also act as a resource to parents by helping them resolve child-rearing issues and answering questions. There are many ways to conduct parent conferences. Following are some helpful planning tips:

- Teachers can send a note home or place a sign-up sheet in a "parent pocket" or in the classroom, to help remind parents of the conference. Many teachers include a brief form requesting parents to identify the issues they would like to see addressed at the conference. This helps to prepare parents and gives them a sense their input is valued and that the conference itself is a valuable part of the program.

- Teachers should think through what they will cover before the conference takes place. It is often helpful to review past observations of the child, think of one or two classroom experiences, or use an assessment tool or progress report to provide parents with an overview of their child's development.

- The tone of a conference should be positive. Conferences are done for all children in the class, not just the ones who are having problems. Conferences should be an avenue to help parents share in their child's school experiences and to impart to the parent how important their child is to the staff and the group of children he or she attends child care with. Conferences are a time to look at the progress and positive growth of the child and to gain important information from parents.

- Give parents something to take home with them. Some teachers provide a special piece of the child's artwork. Others give written observations, copies of assessment tools, or progress reports.

FAMILY NIGHTS are planned events that offer parents and children the opportunity to enjoy child care events together. Family Night might be spaghetti dinner for a classroom or the entire center. It could be a carnival, a holiday party, a staff appreciation party, a children's art show, or a potluck dinner. Events need not be planned often. Once or twice a year can bring parents together to enjoy and celebrate the wonder of each child and family!

A **PARENT NEWSLETTER** can be published weekly, monthly, or whenever there is time to do it! The newsletter might include updates of center and community events, book reviews, parenting articles, notes from the director, classroom updates, amusing stories about children, or announcements of "graduations" to new rooms. Such things as achievements of children (i.e., "toddler Sarah can walk up the slide steps. Hurray for Sarah!")and recognizing parents (i.e., thank-you to Jane's dad, Paul, for repairing the toddler swing) can also be included. Parents can be invited to submit articles, too, if they desire.

A **PARENT ADVISORY COMMITTEE** can be organized in many different ways. In some centers, parents are elected to a committee, which in turn assists the director in making decisions directly affecting the center. In other centers, parents volunteer to serve on the committee and give input and advice to the director or owner at their request. Parent advisory committees may also be responsible for fund-raising efforts, organizing parenting programs, helping with the newsletter, or fixing broken equipment.

A **PARENTING RESOURCE LENDING LIBRARY** can be developed on a large or small scale. Parents can use this convenient library to access books, magazines, and articles. A bulletin board for posting notices and sharing resources, ideas, and events might also be available. Parents should be encouraged to bring additional resources to include in the library.

PARENTING SEMINARS can be designed to meet parents' interests. Classes might be offered on discipline, balancing work and family, or child development. The center can organize the programs and offer them to parents for a fee or free of charge. Center personnel can lead classes, or an outside expert might be asked to present.

Teach Parents How To Participate

Although most parents would like to be a part of their child's program, many do not know how to go about it. While one parent may like spending time in the classroom, another might be more comfortable baking cookies for the annual bake sale. Here are some tips for working with parents:

1. Write down the ways a parent might become involved in your program. Review this in your initial orientation meeting and include it in the parent handbook. The list might include: involvement with an advisory committee, volunteering in the classroom, helping with field trips, editing the newsletter, or organizing parent programs. Ask parents what they might like to do.

2. During parent gatherings, assign a host or hostess in each room to introduce parents new to the program to other, more established parents. Take steps to help them meet mothers and fathers who are already involved in helping at the center. Teachers can take the lead in introducing new parents to one another.

3. Work with staff on how they can deal more effectively with parents.

4. For parents who wish to volunteer in the classroom, prepare a sheet that gives them essential information (i.e., classroom rules, discipline techniques, where to find materials, layout of room). Ensure a positive experience for parents by assigning them to simple tasks or activities with only a few children at a time.

Good parent relations are contingent upon the atmosphere that is pervasive at the center. A respectful attitude toward parents begins at the top! Discourage staff gossip about families and model respectful attitudes toward parents. Staff members build rapport with parents when they greet them by name, share experiences with them about the child's day, and encourage them to feel a part of the program. This rapport, in turn, fosters increased respect from parents for early childhood staff and the overall program.

Parents as Consumers of Child Care Services

As the quality of child care becomes a national issue, parents are taking more responsibility in determining what type of program is best for their child and selecting care based on their research.

Resource and Referral agencies, among other groups, spend a great deal of time helping parents become informed consumers. These agencies are not doing this to make your life more difficult. They know the knowledgeable parent is also the parent who has respect for early childhood professionals and realistic expectations of the value of child care services. In addition, parents who are well informed about choosing the most appropriate care setting for their family will be likely to have a higher degree of satisfaction with the program they choose.

Many parents who are looking for child care will wish to visit the center before placing their child. They may request a personal interview with you. Be prepared for them to ask you many questions; be willing to answer them in an open and enthusiastic manner. If you don't, your competition will!

Questions Parents Ask

- Do you have a written mission statement, including the goals and objectives you have for children?
- How are your teachers screened and hired (with respect to personality, work experience, interest in working with young children, and knowledge of child development)?
- Are your teachers trained? Is on-going training offered or encouraged? Can you tell me about a typical teacher's educational background and experience level?
- Will you review a typical daily schedule?
- Is there a planned curriculum for each classroom? May I see a lesson plan for the class my child will be entering?
- How do staff members discipline children?
- How are parents kept informed about their child's experiences in child care?
- What is the average length of stay for your teachers?
- What is your teacher-to-child ratio?
- Have you had any licensing violations?
- Can I look over your weekly menus?
- Do you or your staff belong to any professional organizations?

If you have written materials to give to parents after their visit, the program stays fresh in their minds and their impression of your center is a positive one. Set a time, perhaps two weeks or a month, after a visit to re-contact the parent. Use this opportunity to clarify procedures and address any of their unanswered questions. This contact can be made personally or over the phone.

Handling Problem Parents

THE DISSATISFIED PARENT: In every center there is always at least one parent who complains about everything. If after taking steps to resolve his or her concerns, you simply are unable to satisfy this parent no matter what you do, it may be best to suggest that another center could better meet their needs.

THE UNCOOPERATIVE PARENT: This is the mother or father who never seems to pay the bill on time or bring diapers for the baby. They consistently pick their children up late and send their children to school sick. Uncooperative parents must be dealt with fairly but directly. Keep a written record of concerns that you have discussed with them. When a parent continues to be negligent regarding policies, follow up with a written reminder stating the consequence for continuous policy violation. When policies are clear and concise, parents run out of acceptable excuses. If policies continue to be violated after meeting with the parent and attempting to resolve the problem, you have the right to ask them to leave the center.

THE PARENT OF A DIFFICULT CHILD: When a child is unruly and dangerous to other children in the classroom and is burning out staff, it may be beneficial to all involved to find a program that better meets the child's individual special needs. This does not relieve child care operators and the child's parent of first exhausting other means. Perhaps outside therapy, management in the classroom, or parent conferences—would resolve the problem and keep the child in the classroom. Try these before making a decision to have his or her parents seek other care.

Dealing with Parent's Concerns

The following points may offer insight into your interactions with parents.

- When a parent appears to be angry, he or she is often masking a deep concern about their child.
- Parents are often quite unsure about their ability to parent.
- Parents almost always have the child's best interests in mind.
- A parent's background and upbringing will affect their values and behaviors.
- Resolution is most acceptable when it is done through mutual problem-solving.
- Get all of the facts from all people involved before taking a position or committing yourself.
- Do not play therapist; don't promote dependent relationships; be available as a resource and source of referral.
- Do not be uncomfortable with seeking outside help on problems that are beyond your area of expertise.
- Be sensitive to parents' concerns, but remember to support your staff and show respect for their professional abilities.

SELF EVALUATION:
Is Your Center Parent-Friendly?

Q: Do you know the names of all your parents? Do you greet them by name when you see them?

Q: Do you also know the names of their children and talk with parents about what's happening at school?

Q: Are you available to talk with parents when they have concerns and problems? Do you respond to their request to meet with you within a day or two?

Q: Does someone greet the parent when he or she comes to pick up the child? Is the greeting positive and welcoming or negative and judgmental?

Q: Is there an effective communication system for parents to get information?

Q: Do you help parents identify resources in the community when they need special services? Do they know you will help?

Q: If problems arise with a child, are the parents involved in resolving the problems?

Q: If your parent population speaks more than one language, is your information available in those languages?

Q: Are your policies on sick children, schedule of operation, fees clear and concise? Do all parents have access to these policies? Have policies been reviewed with parents prior to enrolling their children at the center?

Q: Do you encourage parents to drop in whenever they have the chance? Do you offer them the opportunity to spend time in the classroom, on field trips, or doing special activities?

Q: Do you expect them to be involved with their children's early childhood care and education and support them in this direction?

Q: Is there a mechanism through which parents can give and get formal or informal feedback on child care policies, plus changes affecting them and their children?

Q: Do you demonstrate that you value and respect their children and stress the importance of the children's experiences in your center?

12

Establishing Center Policies

Policies will be different for every center. A campus child care center may have rules limiting use of their program to students, faculty, and staff; they may have unique registration schedules to coincide with the campus calendar year. A parent cooperative may have policies relating to children and parents that another center would not. Most centers have policies that include statements on the following:

General Information

This overall view of a center should cover in detail policies relating to the educational philosophy and goals, number of children, hours of operation, and days when closed. Policy statements will also be needed regarding staff members, opportunities for parental involvement, overview of staff, meal service for children, schedules for children, philosophy of discipline, drop-off and pickup procedures, and the release of children. Other considerations include field trips, insurance coverage, emergency medical release, medications, medical conditions, ill children, and child abuse.

- **REGISTRATION or ENROLLMENT**: This statement should detail when and how parents may enroll their children, the ages of children served, who is eligible to enroll, and enrollment options (i.e., part-time, full-time, extended hour and drop-in care).

- **BILLING INFORMATION**: Billing information should cover several topics including fees, tuition rates, when fees must be paid, how payment agreements can be negotiated, and in what form the payment should be made (check, cash, credit card). It should also address use of multi-child discounts, fees for returned checks, acceptance of Social Service payments for subsidized care, disenrollment for non-payment, absences, vacations, late payments, penalties for late pick-up, and termination agreement.

- **CLASSROOM POLICIES**: Often teachers develop their own set of policies that respond to their own needs and educational orientation. Policies are often formed on the use of blankets, "cuddlies," toys from home, and requests from parents regarding children's birthdays and holidays. Clothing, toothbrushing, special diets, naps, field trips, parent donations, diapers, and toilet training are other policies that may vary from classroom to classroom.

Sample Policies

Following are some sample child care policies which can provide a basic guideline for you in developing your own set of policies. This should not be mistaken for a legal guide to policy design, nor does it represent definitive policies. These are examples only!

General Information

Educational philosophy:

Our program is designed to meet each child's needs, to foster development of competence in intellectual and social skills, and to provide a safe, nurturing environment. Curriculum is developed through extensive assessment, the identification of individual and group goals, and planning of appropriate activities. Our strong commitment to working with parents is evidenced through parent activities and programs.

Program Description:

XYZ Center provides a high quality early education and care program. We are open between the hours of 7:00 A.M. and 6:00 P.M., Monday through Friday. The center serves children aged six weeks to six years and has the capacity to serve 150 children. The center is divided into one infant, two toddler, three preschool, and one kindergarten classroom.

Staff:

The administrative staff at XYZ Center is comprised of a director, assistant director, and administrative assistants.

Each classroom has a supervising teacher, assisting teacher, classroom aide and hourly aides. Supervising teachers are responsible for the over-all daily management of the program and are in the classroom from 7:00 A.M. to 3:00 P.M. Assisting teachers are in the classroom from 10:00 A.M. to 6:00 P.M.

Staff qualifications and child/teacher ratios always meet and often exceed local and state requirements. Our staff is always available to discuss any special needs or concerns you may have. In addition to our regular staff, we also have medical personnel on call for consultations.

Parent Involvement:

Parent involvement is encouraged. Your child will benefit most from our program if parents and staff communicate regularly in both formal meetings and informal conversation. By working together we can design a program that will respond to the individual needs of your child. You are welcome to observe and participate in your child's classroom whenever you wish. We encourage you to feel a part of the center by getting involved in our parent programs.

Holidays:
XYZ Center will be closed on the following holidays:
New Year's Day   Labor Day
President's Day   Thanksgiving Day
Memorial Day   Christmas Day
Fourth of July

NOTE: You are responsible for paying for all holidays the center is closed.

XYZ Center may close due to inclement weather. If the decision is made to close center, parents will be notified and expected to pick up their children as soon as possible.

Arrival and Departure; Release of children:

We ask you to sign your child in and out each day. Sign-in sheets are located near the entrance. Your child will be released only to parents and persons for whom the center has written authorization.

Proper identification is required. This authorization must be left at the front desk. We ask that you notify the classroom as well.

Discipline:

We use several disciplinary techniques which help children to internalize rules and become self-directed in their behavior. These include giving choices, problem solving, natural and logical consequences, ignoring, redirecting, and "cooling off" periods. Additional information on discipline is available in the Parent Resource Library or from your classroom teachers.

We request that parents do not spank their children in the center. We work with children to help them find alternatives to responding physically in stressful situations and strive to make the center a safe place where hitting is not acceptable. It is confusing to children to see that there are exceptions to the rules in school.

Meals and Snacks:

A full-service kitchen operates on the premises and provides breakfast, lunch, and afternoon snacks. All meals are homemade, nutritious, and are served family style. Meals are included in tuition prices. Please check with the Director if your child has any food allergies to see what menu accommodations can be made. Weekly menus are posted on the kitchen bulletin board.

Reporting of suspected child abuse or neglect:

It is our intent to build a partnership with parents to help them provide the most suitable environment possible for children. Toward this goal, we have many resources and referrals available to parents upon request. It is important, also, for parents to be aware that state laws require that any and all incidents of suspected child abuse or neglect be reported to the appropriate agency. It is the responsibility of this agency to investigate each reported case.

Health Information:

In order to maintain a healthy environment, we ask that you not bring your child to school if he/she is showing signs of illness. If your child becomes ill during center hours, you will be contacted immediately and requested to pick him/her up.

You will be contacted if your child shows any of the following symptoms:
- a temperature of over 100 degrees (orally)
- discharge from ears

- discharge from eyes or red eyes
- vomiting or diarrhea lasting over several hours
- any rash or skin lesion that blisters
- excessive signs of cold, tiredness, sore throat, runny nose, sneezing, or coughing.

Medication:

State law requires a prescription for all medicines that are to be administered in a school facility. Over the counter products—such as Tylenol, aspirin, cough syrup, Desitin—may be administered only with a note from a physician. All prescription medication must be in the original container bearing the name of the medicine, date filled, pharmacy label and number, physician's name, child's name, and directions for dosage. In addition, medication will be dispensed only upon your written order.

Medical conditions:

It is important that you inform staff of any special food allergies or medical conditions your child has. This will assist us in being better prepared to handle any emergencies that may arise.

Emergency procedures:

Parents will be contacted immediately in the event of an emergency. Please keep the front office updated of changes in your business and home address and phone numbers so you can be easily located. If other listed contact people cannot be reached, we will call the physician specified by you on the health record form. In case of serious emergency, the closest hospital will be used via an ambulance service.

Registration Enrollment

Enrollment:

Enrollment is open to all children between the ages of six weeks and six years whose needs can be met by XYZ Center. We encourage parents to visit our center with their children to meet our staff, observe in the classrooms, and obtain enrollment forms.

Registration:

You may register your child on a full-time (7:00 A.M. to 6:00 P.M., five days per week) basis. If your child is over 12 months of age, you may arrange for care on a part-time schedule. All children under the age of 12 months must be registered on a full-time basis. In addition, for the kindergarten program, children must be registered for a minimum of five half-day sessions per week.

Drop-in hours:

Drop-in is the addition of hours to a regular schedule. It is important you adhere to your registered hours unless drop-in arrangements have been made with the classroom teacher in advance. Please fill in a drop-in sheet for prior approval.

Billing Information

PAYMENT AGREEMENTS:

If there is a problem with your account or if you will not be able to pay on the due date, please talk with the Director *before* the bill is due. If you are unable to pay your bill on the due date, you may ask for a payment agreement stating when you will pay the amount due. Payment agreements may be for a one-time situation or to change the normal due date to a different time in the month on an ongoing basis.

DISENROLLMENT FOR NONPAYMENT:

Any account not paid by the third working day after it is due, or any payment agreement not paid on the due date, will be sent a past due notice. Children will be dis-enrolled if an account is 10 days past due.

RETURNED CHECKS:

If a check is returned, you will be assessed a $15.00 returned check fee. If the amount is not paid, disenrollment procedures will be initiated. After two returned checks, the client must pay on a cash basis.

SOCIAL SERVICE PAYMENTS:

If your child care is paid for by a government or community agency, please be advised that the late fees for children at the center after 6:00 P.M. and extra hours are not covered. We request you have your caseworker send all contract information to the center. Parental fees must be paid on a timely basis.

ABSENCE CREDITS:

You may receive an absence credit of 50% for illness if your child has missed a week or more from the center. The absence credit may not be used for more than two occasions of illness in a calendar year without approval of special circumstances by the director.

VACATION CREDITS:

XYZ Center does not give credit for any vacation time.

LATE FEES:

Center hours are from 7:00 A.M. to 6:00 P.M. After 6:00 P.M., a late fee of $1.00 per minute will be charged for children remaining at the center after closing. This is strictly enforced.

Classroom Policies

BIRTHDAYS:

Parents are encouraged to allow their child to share his/her birthday with the class. Please give the teacher a few days notice. The teacher will let you know how many children will be at snack time and when to come.

BLANKETS AND CUDDLIES:

Children are encouraged to bring special blankets and cuddlies from home if they wish. All items should be clearly labeled with your child's name.

CLOTHING AND OUTDOOR PLAY:

Children should be dressed in sturdy, comfortable clothing suitable for play. Please mark all clothing with child's name. Each child needs a set of spare clothing at all times. Children spend time outdoors each day and should have appropriate outdoor wear: hats, scarves, snow pants, boots, gloves, coats, and mittens for winter, and comfortable shoes, sunscreen, light clothing for summer.

FIELD TRIPS:

Classrooms often take walks in the vicinity around the center. Parents will be informed prior to any off-campus field trips taken by vehicle. All children traveling in a vehicle will be in seat belts or car seats. Parents are invited to participate in outings.

FOOD:

We ask that all candy, gum, soda, and other edibles be kept at home. If you wish to bring in additional food for lunch or snack, please check with your child's teacher and plan to bring a sufficient supply for your child's entire group.

PARENT DONATIONS:

We welcome donations of almost any kind! Things you throw away can often be used in the classroom. Suggestions include: egg cartons, dishwashing soap and bleach containers, soap cartons, juice cans, old sponges, toilet paper and paper towel rolls.

TOOTHBRUSHING:

Please feel free to provide your child with a child-sized toothbrush for brushing after lunch. Toothpaste donations are always appreciated!

TOYS:

We request that you check with teachers before you allow toys to be brought to school. Sharing personal toys is difficult for young children. Also, we cannot be responsible if a toy is lost or broken.

Classroom teachers ask that "adventure toys" (such as super heros, toy guns) not be brought into the classrooms as these toys are often associated with aggressive play.

DIAPERS:

Parents must supply their children's diapers. There should be at least eight, labeled, in their cubbies at all times.

TOILET TRAINING:

If your child is in the process of toilet training, two or three pairs of underwear and pants will need to be left in his/her cubby. The center's approach toward toilet training is one of positive reinforcement and encouragement. Children are not pushed or shamed into using the toilet. By the age of 2 1/2 to 3 years, we find most children no longer require diapers and are using the toilet regularly.

13

Support Groups

In the growing world of child care, many support groups have been formed for the purpose of assisting and strengthening networks of early childhood professionals. They come in many different shapes and sizes with a wide range of missions and services. There are national level support groups as well as local organizations. At the national level, you will find two major associations for early childhood educators and providers of child care services:

National Association for the Education of Young Children was founded in 1926 in an effort to improve the quality of services to children during the critical years from birth to eight years through professional development opportunities for early childhood educators. With a network of more than 62,000 members in 380 local affiliate groups, NAEYC is a well-respected leader on a wide range of issues relevant to early childhood.

NAEYC members receive the bi-monthly professional journal, *Young Children*, and have access to a wide range of NAEYC published educational resources. A free list of NAEYC publications is available upon request.

NAEYC members are also eligible for reduced registration fees at their annual national conferences. These conferences feature renowned speakers, a wide variety of pertinent workshops, exhibits and displays, film previews, and tours of local facilities. They also encourage networking opportunities among others in the child care profession.

For membership information, contact NAEYC at 1834 Connecticut Avenue, NW, Washington, DC 20009-5786. Their toll-free number is 1-800-424-2460.

The **National Child Care Association** (NCCA) was established to assist child care professionals in business aspects related to child care. Established primarily by proprietary child care organizations, the NCCA is open to all providers of child care services in a center-based setting. The group works to achieve three basic goals: to promote licensed center-based care through public awareness; to assist public and private standard-setting bodies in the development of laws, regulations, and policies affecting child care services; and to expand the availability of licensed child care services.

This organization can be a vital asset in locating available resources and gaining a greater perspective of the overall child care situation. For more information about NCCA, contact P.O. Box 161206, Austin, TX 78716-1206, or call their toll-free number at 1-800-534-7161.

On a local level you will find:
State Associations for the Education of Young Children Groups

The NAEYC has affiliate groups throughout the country. Most states have state associations such as the Colorado Association for the Education of Young Children or the New York Association for the Education of Young Children. Within a particular state, there may be local affiliate groups divided by district or region. These local affiliates often offer a resource to early childhood professionals by providing technical assistance, educational opportunities, peer interaction, and group advocacy efforts.

Director's Networks

Many local communities have a center director's network which offers the opportunity for directors to discuss their challenges and concerns in running a child care program and get feedback on administrative policies. It can be very therapeutic to discover you are not the only center director whose van has just broken down again!

Child Care Center Associations

The NCCA is comprised of a diverse group of individual state organizations that deal with the management of child care facilities. State associations are quite varied in their organizational structure and the types of support services they provide their membership. Whether your state association is highly organized and active, or in an early stage of development, it should be a valuable source of basic information on the status of child care in your area.

Government Agencies

Many local governmental entities (cities, counties, or parishes) have established divisions dealing with child care. These divisions are often called the Office of Children, Office of Families and Children, or Office of Child Care Initiatives. These agencies can provide information about the licensing procedure, local child care legislation, and community child care resources.

Advocacy Groups

As child care begins to take on a visibly important role for families, employers, and government, many groups have been formed at the local level to deal with child care advocacy. Children are often viewed as a population without a voice. These groups have taken it upon themselves to speak on behalf of children and issues affecting children. Your local Department of Social Service or Resource and Referral Agency can give you information about these kinds of organizations.

The Importance of Support Groups

As you can see, there are many people involved in the provision, regulation, and promotion of child care. As a prospective owner or director, you are encouraged to seek them out. As child care in America changes, state and national associations are working hard to respond to those changes, represent their membership, and offer those working in the early childhood field the camaraderie and kinship of a shared profession—caring for young children.

Additional National Resources

These resources can provide valuable support services, networking opportunities, information, and resources to child care providers interested in public policy and advocacy efforts:

The Association of Child Advocates
Building 31, 2nd Floor
3615 Superior Avenue
Cleveland, OH 44114

Association for Childhood Education International
11141 Georgia Avenue, Suite 200
Wheaton, MD 20902
(301) 942-2443

Bank Street College of Education
610 West 112th Street
New York, NY 10025
(212) 663-7200

The Center for the Study of Public Policies for Young Children
High/Scope Education Research Foundation
600 North River Street
Ypsilanti, MI 48197

The Child Care Action Campaign
P.O. Box 313
New York, NY 10185
(212) 334-9595

Child Care Employee Project
P.O. Box 5603
Berkeley, CA 94705

Child Care Information Exchange
P.O. Box 2890
Redmond, WA 98073
(206) 883-9394

Child Care Law Center
625 Market Street, Suite 815
San Francisco, CA 94105
(415) 495-5498

The Children's Defense Fund
122 C Street, NW
Washington, DC 20001
(202) 628-8787

Children's Foundation
815 15th Street
Washington, DC 20005
(202) 347-3300

Family Resource Coalition
230 North Michigan Avenue, Suite 1625
Chicago, IL 60601
(312) 726-4750

National Black Child Development Institute
1463 Rhode Island Avenue, NW
Washington, DC 20515
(202) 387-1281

School Age Child Care Project
Center for Research on Women
Wellesley College
Wellesley, MA 02181
(617) 431-1453

National Association of Child Care Resource and Referral Agencies
2116 Campus Drive, SE
Rochester, MN 55904
(507) 287-2020

Select Committee on Children, Youth, and Families
U.S. House of Representatives
House Annex II, Room 385
Washington, DC 20515

Wheelock College
200 The Riverway
Boston, MA 02215
(617) 743-5200, Ext. 211

Work/Family Directions
Nine Galen Street
Watertown, MA 02172
(800) 346-1535

14

Ask the Experts

The profession of child care is rich with experienced providers, educators, directors, and advocates. Recognizing the depth of expertise from around the country, the authors contacted a diverse group of professionals asking them to identify a pressing concern facing new owners and directors of child care facilities. Following are their responses.

TOPIC: How To Get A License

QUESTION: How can I get a child care license with a minimum amount of red tape, aggravation, and frustration?

ANSWER: 1. Know the rules and regulations inside and out.
           2. Make personal contact with representatives from all licensing agencies, at least by phone, to engage them in a joint collaborative effort.
           3. Have a layout plan and blueprints (for larger centers) ready when you visit agencies.
           4. Keep organized (you may be the only person seeing the whole picture).
           5. *Document* what each inspector has told you and let them know you are doing this.
           6. Be patient.
           7. Be ready to respectfully disagree with requests that are not written in the regulations.

EXPERT: Martha Daley
TITLE: Director
ORGANIZATION: Office of Child Care Initiatives, Denver, CO

TOPIC: Running Your Business

QUESTION: Must I run my child care center as a business since I'm
             doing this because of my interest in children and their
             environment?

ANSWER: Absolutely! That's the key to remaining in a position
             to take care of those children you value. Your first
             priority is to remain a viable concern, and the way to
             survive is to establish sound business practices. Use
             professional help. Consult an attorney to set up the
             proper structure, which, for liability reasons, may be a
             corporate structure. Establish accepted accounting
             practices with the aid of an accountant. Educate your-
             self on insurance, labor laws, and tax matters.
             The list could go on and on. All of this is in addition to
             being totally versed on child care rules and regulations
             your state will have, which certainly impact the cost of
             doing business. Conscientious adherence to sound
             business practice will lead to good management ver-
             sus simply working hard and "taking what comes."

EXPERT: Carolyn Abbot
TITLE: Executive Director
ORGANIZATION: Child Motivation Centers, Lakewood, CO

TOPIC: Marketing

QUESTION: How can I market my center on a limited budget?

ANSWER: The key to marketing your child care center to pro-
             spective customers and the community on a limited
             budget is to plan and implement a mix of activities that
             extend marketing dollars, while positioning you as an
             expert and differentiating you from your competition.
             In addition to advertising, integrate public relations,
             community involvement, and customer relations ac-
             tivities and events into your marketing plan.

For example, before placing an advertisement for a grand opening, join a local business organization, such as the chamber of commerce. Also initiate a referral program for parents and staff, and contact the media to interview you as an expert on a child care topic, such as separation or what constitutes quality child care. Then, when your advertisement is placed, it will have far greater reach, impact, and response than communicating your message through advertising alone. With an integrated marketing approach, the actual dollar investment isn't much more, but the results of your marketing will be significantly better. Remember, marketing sets the stage for good selling. It will not secure enrollment. Only you can do that. How? By having a quality program, an inviting facility, competent staff, and using good personal selling skills.

EXPERT: Julie Wassom
TITLE: President
ORGANIZATION: The Julian Group, Denver, CO

TOPIC: Enrollment Contracts

QUESTION: Should a child care center have a formal enrollment contract with parents?

ANSWER: A formal enrollment contract has a number of advantages for any child care center. First, it *informs* parents exactly what the center's policies are with respect to hours of operation, tuition payments, late fees, closing policies, and other matters. Second, by requiring each parent to sign the contract, it allows the center to avoid misunderstandings before they occur. Third, by requiring a contract, parents will feel more bound by their agreement and more likely to discharge their responsibilities. Fourth, in the event of any dispute, the contract will provide the center with the best evidence of what has been agreed. A formal contract need *not* require that parents stay at the center for a specified length of time. It may allow for termination with a specified notice period.

EXPERT: Mark L. Rosenberg, Esq.
TITLE: Partner
ORGANIZATION: Law firm of Gordon, Feinblatt, Rothman,
                       Hoffberger & Hollander Co-Founder of The
                       Kid's Place, Inc., Chevy Chase, MD

TOPIC: Insurance

QUESTION: How much insurance coverage should I buy for my
            center and what coverages are important?

ANSWER: The best answer is not to try and answer this question
            on your own. You are a child care expert, trained in
            your field. To solve your insurance needs, you should
            select an independent agent who has expertise in the
            field of child care. Choose an independent agent be-
            cause they will work on your behalf and not as an
            employee of an insurance company. Find someone
            with expertise in child care because there are many
            different disciplines in insurance and it is important
            the agent understand your industry and its problems.
            The Independent Insurance Agents (IIA), or Profes-
            sional Insurance Agents (PIA), are associations that
            could help you in the selection of an insurance agency
            with these qualifications.

EXPERT: Brook Mahoney, ARM
TITLE: President
ORGANIZATION: Cherry Creek Insurance Agency, Inc.
                       Englewood, CO

TOPIC: Security

QUESTION: As a child care center operator, how can I assure
            families that their child or children cannot be picked
            up or kidnapped by an unauthorized person?

ANSWER: Safety and security of the children in your care is the
            number one priority in operating a child care center.
            Prior to opening a child care center, you should consult
            with experts to set up a secure system which would
            account for all children in your center at all times. This

system must assure that all center staff are knowledgeable of who has the authority to bring children to the center and pick them up.

EXPERT: Robert D. Rease
TITLE: Educational Specialist
ORGANIZATION: Head Start Bureau; Administration for Children, Youth and Families, Office of Human Development Services/Dept. of Health & Human Services., Denver, CO

TOPIC: Playgrounds

QUESTION: What constitutes adequate playground space, what are considerations for a child care playground, and is a playground really necessary or just another government requirement?

ANSWER: Quality, appropriate outdoor play areas are critical parts of child care facilities. As children spend more time inside, more time in front of the television, and more time sitting by computers, we must provide many opportunities for outdoor play. While your local licensing and health/safety agencies provide minimum requirements, a good program will research information from books. Other programs hire consultants before they design their outdoor play areas. Do not rely soley on information from commercial playground companies.

EXPERT: Francis Wardle, Ph.D.
TITLE: Director
ORGANIZATION: Adams County Head Start/Day Care Commerce City, CO

TOPIC: Staff Evaluations

QUESTION: What kind of evaluation system should I set up for my staff?

ANSWER: Evaluations for staff members occur on two different levels. First and foremost, staff members need a formal assessment twice annually. This evaluation is a combination of a self evaluation by the staff member and observations and insights gathered by the director. The information is shared by both, with specific goals and areas of improvement set (along with specific accomplishments noted). Then a follow-up evaluation is set approximately a month later to assess how the staff member is progressing.

Second, staff members need more informal daily/ weekly feedback from the director, other staff members, parents, and, of course, the children. The feedback is more varied, ranging from a quick pat on the back to an across-the-playground flying hug from a child.

EXPERT: Jean Huntoon Bressor
TITLE: Director of Child Care Programs
ORGANIZATION: Visiting Nurse Association, Burlington, VT

TOPIC: Child care as a living

QUESTION: Can I make a living operating a child care center?

ANSWER: Yes, but it is a difficult endeavor. You must remain flexible in your programing, scheduling, and marketing. Plan to meet parent's needs and answer their concerns. These are the keys to success in the child care center business.

EXPERT: David Pierson
TITLE: Editor & Publisher
ORGANIZATION: Child Care Review, P.O. Box 578, Monterey, Louisiana

TOPIC: Public Policy and Advocacy

QUESTION: How can I become an advocate on child care issues?

ANSWER: In most communities child care providers have organized a number of local and state advocacy organizations, such as Associations of Child Care Centers, Family Child Care Providers, and chapters of the

National Association for the Education of Young Children. Various coalitions are becoming increasingly involved in affecting public policy. Ask other child care professionals or contact your state licensing office to find out how you can join in the advocacy efforts.

EXPERT: Grace Hardy
TITLE: Early Childhood Educator and Advocate
            Denver, CO

TOPIC: Infant and Toddler Care

QUESTION: With such a great need for infant and toddler child care facilities, why don't more centers care for children of this age?

ANSWER: Although the need for infant and toddler care is well documented, the costs for providing this type of care are considerably higher than the costs of providing other types of care. Many states have regulations which require a lower ratio of caregiver to child for this age group, plus square footage requirements for infant and toddler classrooms are often much higher than the square footage requirements for older children. Additionally, the qualifications of the staff caring for infants and toddlers are necessarily more strict, resulting in a higher salary base for staff members of this younger age group. The list goes on. Generally speaking, the regulatory requirements for the care of children of this age are much more restrictive and much more costly.

On the other side of the scale, parents are generally unwilling to pay child care fees of a sufficient amount to cover these costs except in isolated instances. Many child care centers open facilities for a very limited number of infants and toddlers in order to appear as a well rounded program that accepts children of all ages. Many other centers simply choose not to care for children of this age because of the financial risk involved.

EXPERT: Judy Lovin, R.N.
TITLE: Infant and Toddler Child Care Specialist and
                 Consultant, San Francisco, CA

TOPIC: Funding

QUESTION: Where can I get the funds to start my child care center?

ANSWER: In most cases, the financial resources for starting a child care center will come from the individual, partnership, or nonprofit group involved with the project. Approaching a bank or other lending institution, however, may be the only option available in some circumstances. Some owners have had success in securing loans through their local Small Business Administration or through the Women's Bank in their community.

Occasionally, a "silent" partner is interested in investing a sum of money into a local project. Some localities have industrial revenue bonds that may be utilized for child care businesses. Check with your local economic development office.

Sometimes other financial resources are available to nonprofit organizations in the form of grants from government agencies or private foundations. However, these are almost always associated with a specialized project and rarely include construction costs. One must be diligent in canvassing the Federal Register and annual reports of foundations. In many communities, The Junior League produces a foundation directory identifying sources of funds and funding priorities.

While most government sources of funding do not include program start-up funds, many do provide support for operating expenses. In some parts of the country, a child care fund that provides guaranteed revolving loans, outright grants, or donations of land are available to nonprofit organizations. Contact your local and state government for sources of funds that might be available.

Private businesses are recent sources of funding for child care centers. Companies wishing to offer a child care center as a benefit to their employees may join with other companies in a consortium or cooperative effort to finance the opening of a child care center. In some instances individual companies will even put up the money to open a center at their work site. These companies typically are interested in hiring a child care management group to run the center. Proven track records in fiscal management and operation of a child care center are usually prerequisites for this type of arrangement.

EXPERT: Donna Chitwood
TITLE: Director
ORGANIZATION: Fairfax County Employer Child Care Council
                 Fairfax, VA

TOPIC: Permitting

QUESTION: Once I have identified a site for my child care center, how do I begin the permitting process?

ANSWER: Find out if a single point of entry exists. You might start with your county health department or state department of social services.
Contact appropriate agencies in your city, county, and state governments to obtain the mandated requirements. Agencies typically will include Health Department, Zoning, Environmental Management, Fire & Rescue, Social Services, Office for Children and/or Human Services. The names and numbers of agencies will vary from one location to the next.
In general, first determine whether child care is a permitted use according to the zoning regulations. If the activity is not allowed by right, you may be able to apply for a special use permit. In either case, you will also need to inquire about what special conditions may need to be met before an application will be approved. Next, gather information on the building codes which will apply to this type of activity and age group of children. If you are planning to renovate an existing facility, have the building inspected to find out what plumbing, mechanical, electrical, fire, and other renovations will be required to bring the building up to

mandated codes. If you are going to build a center, building plans will need to be approved. A site plan prepared by a licensed engineer, architect, landscape architect, designer, or land surveyor will need to be submitted for review. The site plan will show the location of the building and specify how requirements are met for conditions such as parking, buffering, landscaping, and drainage.

Following these steps, you will need to obtain building permits, request numerous inspections, and secure the final licensing permit to operate the child care center. Be prepared to pay more than one fee as you go through the permit process. The amount of time to complete the process will vary from one jurisdiction to another. It will take from several months to over a year to open a child care center.

EXPERT: Barbara Dykes
TITLE: Assistant Director
ORGANIZATION: Fairfax County Employer Child Care Council
                     Fairfax, VA

15

Forms To Make Your Job Easier

This easy-to-use, comprehensive forms package provides 30 reproducible forms covering "Health and Safety", "Registration/ Intake", "Observations", "Evaluations", and other topic areas. You may need to modify them to accommodate your center's policies and your state rules and regulations. You'll save time and effort with these field-tested forms.

* Refer to the order blank in back of this book for your ready to use forms kit.

Enrollment Record

Date of enrollment _____

1. Child's name _____ Birthdate _____
   Name by which child is often called _____
   Home address _____ Phone _____
   City _____ Zip _____

2. Mother or Guardian's Name _____
   Address (if different from child) _____
   Place of Employment _____ Business Phone _____

3. Father or Guardian's Name _____
   Address (if different from child) _____
   Place of Employment _____ Business Phone _____

4. Special instructions for contacting parents: _____

5. If neither parent or guardian can be reached in case of emergency _____
   call: _____

6. Child's Doctor: Name _____ Phone _____
   Child's Dentists: Name _____ Phone _____

7. Other Children in Family (Name and Age) _____
   _____

8. Other Adults in Family (Name and Relationship): _____
   _____

9. Previous Child Care Experiences (Locations and Dates) _____
   _____

10. Additional Information Concerning Your Child
    Play Habits _____
    Eating Behavior _____
    Likes and Dislikes _____ Fears _____

Statement of Authorization

I,_____ give my permission to the school
to call a doctor for medical or surgical care for my child_____
_____ should an emergency arise. It is understood
that a conscientious effort will be made to locate us: this expense will be
accepted by us.

_____
Signature   Date

Field Trips

I,_____ give my consent for my
child_____ to take part in field trips or excursions
under proper supervision by the Child Care Center staff. I will contact the
Center in the event I do not wish my child to participate.

_____
Signature   Date

Child Release

I give my consent for my children (child) NAME_____
to be released to the following persons only. In the event I am unable to pick
him/her/them up personally:

1. _____   4. _____
2. _____   5. _____
3 _____   6. _____

_____
Signature   Date

Enrollment Agreement

I have thoroughly read the Parent Handbook of of this child center and am in agreement with the following policies regarding my child's enrollment in the school (center):

1) Tuition is due in Advance
2) Tuition is charged on a weekly basis according to the schedule which I establish for my child. I understand that I am charged full tuition even if my child is absent - unless I've made arrangements with the office for vacation credit.
3) Vacation credit can be taken up to 15 days from Sept. - Sept. provided this request is turned into the office in writing 5 school days in advance of the requested vacation days.
4) Two weeks written notice is required if my child is going to leave the center permanently. If proper notice is not given I will be charged for 2 weeks beyond my child's last day of attendance. Health and academic records will not be released until account is paid in full.
5) A tuition credit of 1/2 of my daily charge will be given for the following holidays: Labor Day, Thanksgiving Day, Presidents Day, Memorial Day, Christmas, New Years and July 4th.
6) There will be a $15.00 charge on all returned checks to cover bookkeeping costs.
7) The center is not responsible for lost or damaged items of clothing or toys.

    _____
    Parent's Signature

    _____
    Date

If collection action is taken on my account, I agree to assume all costs.

HEALTH FORM

Child's Name _____Sex _____Birthdate _____
Street _____ City _____Zip _____
Mother or Guardian's Name_____
Father or Guardian's Name _____
If Tuberculin Test Given: Date _____Result _____

Surgery, Accidents, Illnesses, Chronic or Handicapping Problems:
_____

Physical Findings (Include Vision and Hearing, if Tested):
_____
_____

Recommendations for Health Follow-up in Child Care Settings:
_____
_____

Restrictions:
Activity _____
Diet _____
Other _____

_____
Signature of Physician

Date_____

DAILY SIGN-IN SHEET

	CHILD'S NAME	PARENT'S NAME	TIME IN	TIME OUT	PARENT'S NAME	COMMENTS
1						
2						
3						
4						
5						
6						
7						
8						
9						
10						
11						
12						
13						
14						
15						
16						
17						
18						
19						
20						
21						
22						
23						
24						
25						
26						
27						
28						
29						
30						
31						
32						
33						
34						
35						
36						

Medication Sign-In Sheet

1. Colorado State Law requires a prescription for all medicines that are to be administered in a school facility.
2. Over-the-counter products, such as Tylenol, Aspirin, Cough Syrup, Desitin, etc., may be administered **ONLY** with a note from a physician.
3. All medication must be properly labeled with your child's name.
4. All medication must be stored in the kitchen refrigerator.
5. Please remember to pick up your Child's medication each afternoon.
6. Please do not embarrass yourself or our staff by asking for exceptions to these rules.

Child's Name	Medication	Dosage	Time To Be Given	Parent Signature	Given By	Time Given
1.						
2.						
3.						
4.						
5.						
6.						

FIELD TRIP REPORT

Group Size _____

Attending Teachers

Date _____

_____

Destination _____

_____

_____

Departure Time _____

_____

Expected Arrival _____

Actual Arrival_____

Group Name

1. _____   16. _____

2. _____   17. _____

3. _____   18. _____

4. _____   19. _____

5. _____   20. _____

6. _____   21. _____

7. _____   22. _____

8. _____   23. _____

9. _____   24. _____

10. _____   25. _____

11. _____   26. _____

12. _____   27. _____

13. _____   28. _____

14. _____   29. _____

15. _____   30. _____

_____
Teacher's Signature

INJURY - ACCIDENT REPORT

Child's Name _____

Date _____ Time_____

Description of Injury _____

_____

Location of Incident _____

_____

Circumstances surrounding incident _____

_____

Treatment Administered _____

Treatment Advised _____

_____

Supervising Teacher

_____

Director

application for employment

We are an equal opportunity employer, dedicated to a policy of nón-discrimination in employment on any basis including race, color, age, sex, religion or national origin.

PERSONAL INFORMATION

Date _____

Social Security Number _____

Last

Name _____

Last   First   Middle

Present Address _____

Street   City   State   Zip

Permanent Address _____

Street   City   State   Zip

Phone No. _____

Referred By _____

First

EMPLOYMENT DESIRED

Position _____

Date You Can Start _____

Salary Desired _____

Are You Employed Now? _____

If So May We Inquire of Your Present Employer? _____

Ever Applied to this Company Before? _____   Where _____   When _____

Middle

EDUCATION

	Name and Location of School	Circle Last Year Completed	Did You Graduate?	Subjects Studied and Degree(s) Received
Grammer School			☐ Yes ☐ No	
High School		1 2 3 4	☐ Yes ☐ No	
College		1 2 3 4	☐ Yes ☐ No	
Trade, Business or Correspondence School		1 2 3 4	☐ Yes ☐ No	

Subjects of Special Study or Research Work _____

_____

_____

Activities Other Than Religious (Civic, Athletic, etc.) _____

EXCLUDE ORGANIZATIONS, THE NAME OR CHARACTER OF WHICH INDICATES THE RACE, AGE, SEX, COLOR OR NATIONAL ORIGIN OF ITS MEMBERS.

(Continued on Other Side)

FORMER EMPLOYERS List Below Last Four Employers, Starting With Last One First

Date Month and Year	Name and Address of Employer	Salary	Position	Reason for Leaving
From				
To				
From				
To				
From				
To				
From				
To				

REFERENCES: Give Below the Names of Three Persons Not Related To You, Whom Your Have Known At Least One Year.

	Name	Address	Business	Years Acquainted
1.				
2.				
3.				

PHYSICAL RECORD:

Do you have any physical condition which may limit your ability to perform the job applied for?   This question is voluntary, and any answers will be kept confidential?

In Case of Emergency Notify

Name	Address	Phone No.

I authorize investigation of all statements contained in this application. I understand that misrepresentation or omission of facts called for is cause for dismissal. Further, I understand and agree that my employment is for no definite period and may, regardless of the date of payment of my wages and salary, be terminated at any time without any previous notice.

Date   Signature

DO NOT WRITE BELOW THIS LINE

Interviewed By   Date

REMARKS:

Neatness		Ability	

Hired	For Dept.	Position	Will Report	Salary Wages

Approved: 1.   2.   3.

Employment Manager	Dept. Head	General Manager

STAFF EVALUATION

Date
Name of Employee
Position

1. Knowledge of Job: (Consider extent of person's knowledge of present job: knows what to do and why; increases his/her knowledge of the job)
    ____ Has an exceptionally thorough knowledge of job
    ____ Has good knowledge of work
    ____ Requires considerable coaching
    ____ Has inadequate knowledge of work

2. Quality of Work: (Consider ability to do high quality work: consistency; follow-through)
    ____ Highest quality
    ____ Well done
    ____ Passable
    ____ Poor

3. Quantity of Work: (Consider amount of work completed under normal conditions: produces expected number of projects and activities)
    ____ Large amount
    ____ Good amount
    ____ Slightly below average
    ____ Unsatisfactory

4. Attendance and Punctuality: (Consider frequency of absences as well as lateness)
    ____ Excellent record
    ____ Occasionally late or absent
    ____ Frequently absent or late
    ____ Undependable
    ____ Begins work promptly upon arriving
    ____ Unnecessary delays in starting work

5. Attitude: (Consider attitude toward work, school, associates, and willingness to work with others: pitches in when needed; works well with others; makes effort to understand policies; willing to do less desirable tasks)
___ Excellent cooperation
___ Good cooperation
___ Fair cooperation
___ Poor cooperation

6. Judgment: (Consider ability to make decisions and to utilize working time; plan logically; obtain facts before making decisions; knows when to seek advice; acts wisely in unusual situations)
___ Justifies utmost confidence
___ Needs little supervision
___ Needs frequent checking
___ Needs constant supervision

7. Reliability: (Consider ability to work under pressure and to complete job; retains composure under pressure; completes assignments satisfactorily and on time)
___ Very dependable
___ Generally dependable
___ Unpredictable

8. Personal Characteristics: (Consider manners, grooming and appearance, health, poise, patience, ambition)
___ Very satisfactory
___ Satisfactory
___ Needs improvement in certain areas; specify:

9. Miscellaneous
   Excessive misuse of breaks   yes ___
        no ___

   Excessive personal telephone calls   yes ___
        no ___

10. Suggestions for improvement:

_____
Signature of Employee

_____
Signature of Supervisor

TEACHING STAFF — SELF-EVALUATION FORM

Evaluate your own performance on this form. Please check the appropriate space to the right of each statement.

W = working on it.
M = most of the time.
A = always.

		W	M	A

RELATIONSHIPS

1. I share my positive feelings by arriving with a good attitude.
2. I greet children, parents and staff in a friendly and acceptable manner.
3. I accept suggestions and criticism from my co-workers gratefully.
4. I can handle tense situations and retain my composure.
5. I make an effort to be sensitive to the needs of the children and their parents.
6. I am willing to share my ideas and plans so that I can contribute to the total program.

GOALS

1. I have a classroom that is organized for a quality child care program.
2. I constantly review the developmental stage of each child so that my expectations are reasonable.
3. I set classroom and individual goals and then evaluate regularly.
4. I have fostered independence in my children.
5. I make a conscientious effort to expand my knowledge of good early childhood techniques.
6. I consistently coordinate long-term and short-term goals for the overall improvement of my class program.
7. I participate in in-service training opportunities so that I can improve and enlarge my knowledge.

| | W | M | A |

CLASSROOM SKILLS

1. I arrive on time and ready for the first child.
2. I face each day as a new experience.
3. I plan a balanced program for the children in all skill areas.
4. I am organized and have a plan for the day.
5. I help each child recognize the role of being part of a group.
6. I help children develop friendships.
7. I maintain a child oriented classroom and the bulletin boards enhance the room.
8. Visitors to our classroom are welcome.

PROFESSIONALISM

1. I have been conscientious in my use of sick days.
2. I understand the school philosophy and can share it with parents and community.
3. I have been loyal to the school and director.
4. I do not gossip about the staff and/or families of the students.
5. I maintain professional attitudes in my demeanor and in my personal relationships while on the job.
6. I assume my share of joint responsibilities.
7. I maintain good communications with the director regarding group and center problems.
8. I participate in pertinent school activities outside my regular hours.

PERSONAL QUALITIES

1. I have basic emotional stability.
2. My general health is good and does not interfere with my responsibilities.
3. I strive to maintain professional attitudes and appearances.
4. I stay involved with the children rather than just observing or babysitting them.
5. I set a good healthy model for the children.

_____   _____
Staff signature   Date

_____   _____
Director's signature   Date

STAFF REFERENCE FORM

_____has applied for a position with this child care facility. You were listed as a reference.

We would appreciate a response to the following questions and returning this form as soon as possible. The information which you give us will be used in evaluating this candidate for the position.

How long have you known this person? _____

In what capacity have you known her/him? _____

Why do you feel this person is seeking employment with young children? _____
_____
_____

Do you feel she/he is reliable and dependable? _____
_____

How do you feel she/he relates to young children? _____
_____

How would you rate her/his knowledge of child development? _____
_____

What special skills fo you feel she/he has in working with young children? _____
_____

Would you recommend this person for this position? _____

                                        Sincerely,

_____   _____
Reference Person Signature   Center Director

STAFF HEALTH CERTIFICATE

Name _____

Address _____ Phone _____

City _____ Zip Code _____

Birthdate _____

I have examined the above named person and certify that he/she is:

      1) free from contagious disease
      2) in satisfactory physical condition to have close association with children

Tuberculin Test _____ Results _____
                      date

_____   _____
Date   Physician's Signature

                           _____
                           Address

STAFF TIME SHEET

DATE	TIME IN-OUT	HOURS	BREAKS		DATE	TIME IN-OUT	HOURS	BREAKS

		Checklist for Maintaining Staff Records										Teacher's Name		
												Empl. Date		
												Phys.	Medical	
												T.B.		
												Phys.	Medical Update	
												T.B.		
												#1	Reference	
												#2		
												#3		
												Red Cross		
												W-4		
												Other		
												Term Date		

Dear Parents,

We realize that many of you are experiencing financial difficulties, but it is necessary for us to meet our costs (such as food, rent, staffing, etc.) on a timely basis. In order for us to do that, we need your cooperation in paying for services as they occur.

Payment is due on Monday for the week. A $5.00 late charge will be automatically added to your balance if not paid by Wednesday. If payment is not received by Friday, your child will not be permitted to attend school the following Monday.

Because we are experiencing an increase in late payments recently, we will implement the following policy Monday, _____

Thank You

Director

_____

TUITION REMINDER

Our records indicate that we have not yet received your tuition payment for this week. We need your cooperation in paying for your child care services as they occur. We are bringing this matter to your attention to give you the opportunity to bring your account up to date. A $5.00 late charge is added to all accounts which remain unpaid at 6:00 p.m. Tuesday.

Thank you for giving this your immediate attention.

TUITION NOTICE

Our records indicate that we have not received your tuition payment for this week. Please understand that the continuation of our program depends solely on your cooperation in paying for your child care services as they occur.

Your payment in the amount of $——————— **must** accompany your child before he/she may attend next week.

Dear Parents:

This privilege of serving you has certainly been our pleasure. For this, we extend our sincere thanks.

However, in reviewing our records, we find that your account lists the amount of $_____ that became due some time ago.

We feel certain that you understand how important and necessary it is that all fees for child care services be paid in full. You can help us in this respect by sending us your payment. Your immediate attention to this matter will be greatly appreciated and will, above all, enable us to continue to offer a quality child care program.

Sincerely,

Director

Dear Parents:

You account in the amount of $_____ is long overdue. It is a matter of definite concern to us.

Since we have not received your payment at the time of this mailing, we must inform you that in order to avoid any future financial problems and to avoid a decidedly bad credit rating for your future use as a consumer, it is imperative that you take care of this immediately.

If you are unable to pay the total amount due at this time, we are willing to accept partial payments towards your account. However, if you continue to ignore this matter it will force us to take legal action.

Sincerely,

Director

NOTICE: You have 30 days in which to inform us of any billing errors. A 12% interest rate will be charged on all past due accounts as of 7/1/86.

Dear Parents,

Now that the cold weather has arrived, we would like to remind you to please dress your children appropriately for the weather. With the exception of extremely nasty days, we do have outdoor recreation every day even if for only 10 minutes. Please be sure your children have winter coats, hats, mittens, and boots to keep them warm and dry. If your child wears moon boots, please bring another pair of shoes for he or she to change into. Also please label these items with your child's name to avoid confusion.

We would also like to ask your assistance in gathering a supply of spare clothing! We are in great need of clothing for children who have accidents or perhaps get wet from outside activity. Could you please check your child's closets and drawers for items that they may have outgrown? Long pants, underclothing, shirts, and socks are the most urgently needed items. We are also desperately in need of crib sheets and small blankets. If your child has worn some of our spare clothing home, please try to get them back to us for the next time they are needed. I'll leave a box by the front desk marked Spare Clothing.

Thank you for helping us keep your children dry and comfortable.

FIELD TRIP SCHEDULE FOR JUNE 1989

DATE	DATE	DESTINATION
Thursday	June 2	Lyons Park
Monday	June 6	Wheat Ridge Municipal Pool
Tuesday	June 7	Children's Museum
Wednesday	June 8	Surfside Pool
Thursday	June 9	Putt-Putt Golf
Friday	June 10	Buffalo Bill's Grave-Lookout Mtn.
Monday	June 13	Fire Station
Tuesday	June 14	Red Rocks Park
Wednesday	June 15	Surfside Pool
Thursday	June 16	Speaker from Dumb Friends League
Friday	June 17	Golden Gate Canyon
Monday	June 20	BBQ - Aurora School
Tuesday	June 21	Birthday Party
Wednesday	June 22	Hall of Life
Thursday	June 23	Rollerskating
Friday	June 24	Cherry Creek Reservoir
Monday	June 27	Funtastic
Tuesday	June 28	Rocky Mountain Park
Wednesday	June 29	Surfside Pool
Thursday	June 30	Bus ride Downtown

ANNOUNCING:
We are happy to announce that the tumbling and movement classes will begin again the week of January 14. Our new adventure in creative movement is developing and many of our children have already been involved. This six weeks we will incorporate an additional class which will be mainly tap dancing with a little ballet. Ballet shoes are quite optional but tap shoes are recommended. Taps can be put into regular shoes quite inexpensively. This class will meet on Monday mornings and will be the same low price of $5.00. Tumbling class will meet on Monday and Thursday mornings.

WHAT ARE OUR OBJECTIVES?
By using special techniques and teaching aids, an environment can be created which will develop a positive attitude and imagination. Self-improvement is encouraged by directing the child's energy towards good, challenging activities.

WE WILL WORK TOWARDS DEVELOPING:
- Strength and stamina
- Self-discipline
- Rhythm
- Balance and coordination
- Body awareness
- A positive self image

In order to make these special classes available to all children, we are striving to keep the cost low. One six week session will be $5.00. Please register as soon as possible.

REGISTRATION FORM
Please enroll my child, _____ in:
_____ Tumbling and Creative Movement classes
_____ Tap dancing and Ballet classes

_____ Preschool
_____ Pre-Kindergarten
_____ Kindergarten
_____ Schoolage

Please make checks payable to

Each class is $5.00.

_____
Parent Signature

_____
Phone

Write your own check for $50.00!

As a way of saying **THANK YOU** to all of you who help us spread the good word about this child care center, we'd like to give you $50.00.

Here's how it works!

Tell a friend or 10 friends how much your child enjoys this child care center and how we meet your needs as a working parent. Encourage them to call the school for more information and we'll invite them for a cup of coffee and a look around. When your friend registers their child, you fill in the check below and turn it into the office. After 4 weeks attendance we'll credit your account with $50.00! IT'S THAT EASY! All we want you to do is to tell others why you've chosen this child care center and encourage them to do the same.

Don't delay! The $50.00 is burning a hole in our pockets!

- -

PAY TO THE ACCOUNT OF: _____ **$50.00**

FAMILY REFERRED _____

ENTRANCE DATE _____ CREDIT DATE _____

_____
DIRECTOR SIGNATURE

Dear Parents,

It's time to put the school year behind us and we are making plans for the summer. Check your calendars because we have a summer full of fun and activities planned.

Attached you will find activity sheets for the months of June, July and August.

SCHOOL-AGERS

The activity fee for all school agers is $8.00 per month. This fee will cover admission charges, open swim fees and transportation costs. June fee is due by June 20th. July and August fees are due on the 1st of each month.

KINDERGARTNERS

It is our intention to include all Kindergarten graduates on those field trips that are appropriate for their age. You will be notified by a note on the front door with cost and destination of each trip.

FREE CARNIVAL

Pony Rides
Fun Booths for Kids
Information Booths for Parents
Hot Dogs & Juice
Saturday, May 31st
10 a.m. - 1 p.m.
5205 W. 26th Ave.
Sponsored by this Child Care Center

Kids On The Move!!!

Enjoy making new friends, sharing
experiences and discovering "new" places.
Our Summer Program includes:
Swimming — Dramatics —
Roller Skating — Arts & Crafts
Cooking — Sports — Bowling

Ask About Our Summer Special

XYZ CHILD
CARE CENTER

Dear Parents,

As of September 15, 1986 XYZ centers will assume administrative responsibility for this child care facility. It is our intention to have as smooth a transition as possible. Those changes that do take place we hope you will view as improvements and for the betterment of your child's school program. After managing this facility for 6 years, I am confident that we have a bright future ahead.

Attached please find our current rate sheet. You will notice that our rates are the same for most schedules and we would hope that they remain there for some time. Our payment policy requires that payment be received on Monday for that week of services. Please make every effort to adhere to this policy.

If you currently have a past due balance with ABC Center Academy, please make your payment directly to them. To minimize confusion in this matter, please make a separate payment in an envelope labeled "ABC Center Academy."

I look forward to meeting all of you and working with you in the near future. If you have questions or concerns, please feel free to call me at Ph#_____.

Sincerely,

_____

Director

Form **2441**	Credit for Child and Dependent Care Expenses	OMB No. 1545-0068
Department of the Treasury Internal Revenue Service (O)	▶ Attach to Form 1040. ▶ See Instructions below.	19**88** Attachment Sequence No. **23**
Name(s) as shown on Form 1040		Your social security number

Note: *If you paid cash wages of $50 or more in a calendar quarter to an individual for services performed in your home, you must file an employment tax return. Get Form 942 for details.*

1 Enter number of qualifying persons who were cared for in 1988. (See instructions for definition of qualifying persons.) ▶ ___[1]___
  Caution: *To qualify, the person(s) must have shared the same home with you in 1988.*

2 Enter the amount of **qualified** expenses you incurred and actually paid in 1988 for the care of the qualifying person. (See **What Are Qualified Expenses?** in the instructions.) Do **not** enter more than $2,400 ($4,800 if you paid for the care of two or more qualifying persons) **2**

3a You **must** enter your earned income on line 3a. See line 3 instructions for definition of earned income   **3a**

  b If you are married, filing a joint return for 1988, you must enter your spouse's earned income on line 3b. (If spouse is a full-time student or is disabled, see the line 3 instructions for amount to enter.) . . **3b**

  c If you are married filing a joint return, compare the amounts on lines 3a and 3b, and enter the **smaller** of the two amounts on line 3c **3c**

4   ● If you were unmarried at the end of 1988, compare the amounts on lines 2 and 3a, ⎫
     and enter the **smaller** of the two amounts on line 4.   ⎬ **4**
     ● If you are married filing a joint return, compare the amounts on lines 2 and 3c, and
     enter the **smaller** of the two amounts on line 4.   ⎭

5 Enter decimal amount from table below that applies to the adjusted gross income on Form 1040, line 31   **5**   ×.

If line 31 is:		Decimal amount is:	If line 31 is:		Decimal amount is:
Over—	But not over—		Over—	But not over—	
	$0–10,000	.30	$20,000	22,000	.24
10,000	12,000	.29	22,000	24,000	.23
12,000	14,000	.28	24,000	26,000	.22
14,000	16,000	.27	26,000	28,000	.21
16,000	18,000	.26	28,000		.20
18,000	20,000	.25			

6 Multiply the amount on line 4 by the decimal amount on line 5, and enter the result **6**

7 Multiply any child and dependent care expenses for 1987 that you paid in 1988 by the percentage that applies to the adjusted gross income on your 1987 Form 1040, line 31, or Form 1040A, line 13. Enter the result. (See line 7 instructions for the required statement.) **7**

8 Add amounts on lines 6 and 7. See the worksheet in the instructions for line 8 for the amount of credit you can claim **8**

General Instructions
Paperwork Reduction Act Notice.—We ask for this information to carry out the Internal Revenue laws of the United States. We need it to ensure that taxpayers are complying with these laws and to allow us to figure and collect the right amount of tax. You are required to give us this information.

The time needed to complete and file this form will vary depending on individual circumstances. The estimated average time is:

Recordkeeping	20 minutes
Learning about the law or the form	11 minutes
Preparing the form	16 minutes
Copying, assembling, and sending the form to IRS	17 minutes

If you have comments concerning the accuracy of these time estimates or suggestions for making this form more simple, we would be happy to hear from you. You can write to either IRS or the Office of Management and Budget at the addresses listed in the instructions of Form 1040.

What Is the Child and Dependent Care Expenses Credit?
You may be able to take this credit if you paid someone to care for your child or other qualifying person so you could work or look for work in 1988. The credit may be as much as $720 ($1,440 if two or more qualifying persons were cared for).
Additional Information.—For more details, please get Pub. 503, Child and Dependent Care Credit.

Who Is a Qualifying Person?
A qualifying person is:
● Any person under age 15 whom you claim as a dependent (but see **Children of divorced or separated parents**).
● Your disabled spouse who is mentally or physically unable to care for himself or herself.
● Any disabled person who is mentally or physically unable to care for himself or herself and whom you claim as a dependent, or could claim as a dependent except that he or she had income of $1,950 or more.

Children of divorced or separated parents.—If you were divorced, legally separated, or lived apart from your spouse during the last 6 months of 1988, you may be able to claim the credit even if your child is not your dependent. If your child is not

your dependent, he or she is a qualifying person if all five of the following apply:
1. You had custody of the child for the longer period during the year; and
2. The child received over half of his or her support from one or both of the parents; and
3. The child was in the custody of one or both of the parents over half of the year; and
4. The child was under age 15, or was physically or mentally unable to care for himself or herself; and
5. The child is not your dependent because—
  a. As the custodial parent, you have signed **Form 8332**, or a similar statement, agreeing not to claim the child's exemption for 1988; or
  b. You were divorced or separated before 1985 and your divorce decree or written agreement states that the other parent can claim the child's exemption, and the other parent provides at least $600 in child support during the year. **Note:** *This rule does not apply if your decree or agreement was changed after 1984 to specify that the other parent cannot claim the child's exemption.*

Who May Take the Credit?
To claim the credit, **all five** of the following must apply:

(Continued on back)

Form **2441** (1988)

Forms To Make Your Job Easier

177

Form 2441 (1988)

Page 2

1. You paid for the care so you (and your spouse if you were married) could work or look for work (but see **Spouse who is a full-time student or is disabled**).
2. You and the qualifying person(s) lived in the same home.
3. You (and your spouse if you were married) paid over half the cost of keeping up your home. The cost includes: rent; mortgage interest; property taxes; utilities; home repairs; and food eaten at home.
4. The person you paid to provide the care was not your spouse or a person you could claim as a dependent.
Note: *If you paid your child to provide the care, he or she must have been 19 or older by the end of 1988.*
5. If you were married at the end of 1988, generally, you must file a joint tax return. But you will be treated as unmarried and still be eligible to take the credit if:
   a. You were legally separated; or
   b. You were living apart from your spouse during the last 6 months of the year, the qualifying person lived with you in your home over 6 months, and you provided over half the cost of keeping up your home.

What Are Qualified Expenses?
Qualified expenses include amounts paid for household services and care of the qualifying person while you work or look for work. Child support payments are **not** qualified expenses.
Household services.—These services must be needed to care for the qualifying person as well as to run the home. They include, for example, the services of a cook, maid, babysitter, housekeeper, or cleaning person if the services were partly for the care of the qualifying person. Do not include services of a chauffeur or gardener.
Note: *If you paid cash wages of $1,000 or more for household services in any calendar quarter in 1987 or 1988, you should file a Form 940 for 1988 by January 31, 1989.*
Care of the qualifying person.—Care includes the cost of services for the qualifying person's well-being and protection. It does not include the cost of clothing or entertainment.
You may count care provided outside your home if the care was for your dependent under age 15, or any other qualifying person who regularly spends at least 8 hours a day in your home.
Generally, care does not include food or schooling expenses. However, if these items are included as part of the total care, and they are incident to, and cannot be separated from, the total cost, you may count the total payment. However, you may not count the cost of schooling for a child in the first grade or above, or the expenses for sending your child to an overnight camp.
Medical expenses.—Some dependent care expenses may qualify as medical expenses. If you itemize deductions, you may want to take all or part of these medical expenses on Schedule A (Form 1040). Get Pub. 503 for details.

Specific Instructions
Line 2. Dollar limit.—Enter the amount of qualified expenses you incurred and actually paid in 1988. But the most you may figure the credit on is $2,400 a year for one qualifying person, or $4,800 a year for two or more qualifying persons. Do not

include amounts paid or incurred by your employer to the extent they are excluded from gross income.
Note: *Do not include on line 2 qualified expenses that you incurred in 1988 but did not pay until 1989. Instead, you may be able to increase your 1989 credit when you pay the 1988 expenses in 1989.*
Line 3. Earned income limit.—The amount of your qualified expenses may not be more than your earned income or, if married filing a joint return, the **smaller** of your earned income or your spouse's earned income.
In general, earned income is wages, salaries, tips, and other employee compensation. It also includes net earnings from self-employment. This is usually the amount shown on Schedule SE (Form 1040), line 3 (or 3c if you file section B).
Unmarried taxpayers.—If you were unmarried at the end of 1988 or are treated as being unmarried at the end of the year, enter your earned income on line 3a.
Married taxpayers.—If you are married, filing a joint return, disregard community property laws. Enter your earned income on line 3a and your spouse's earned income on line 3b. Then, enter the smaller of the two incomes on line 3c. If your spouse died in 1988, had no earned income, and you file a joint return for 1988, see Pub. 503.
Spouse who is a full-time student or is disabled.—If your spouse was a full-time student or was mentally or physically unable to care for himself or herself, figure your spouse's earned income on a monthly basis to determine your spouse's earned income for the year. For each month that your spouse was disabled or a full-time student, your spouse is considered to have earned income of not less than $200 a month ($400 a month if more than one qualifying person was cared for in 1988).
If, in the same month, both you and your spouse were full-time students and did not work, you may not use any amount paid that month to figure the credit. The same applies to a couple who did not work because neither was capable of self-care.
A **full-time student** is one who was enrolled in a school for the number of hours or classes that the school considers full time. The student must have been enrolled during each of 5 months during 1988. The months need not be consecutive.
Self-employment income.—You must reduce your earned income by any loss from self-employment. If your net earnings from self-employment are less than $1,600, and you use the optional method to figure your self-employment tax, you may be able to increase your net earnings to $1,600 for this credit. Get **Pub. 533,** Self-Employment Tax, for details. If you only have a loss from self-employment, or your loss is more than your other earned income and you do not use the optional method, you may not take the credit.
Line 7.—If you had qualified expenses for 1987 that you did not pay until 1988, you may be able to increase the amount of credit you may take in 1988. To do this, multiply the 1987 expenses you paid in 1988 by the percentage from the table on line 5 that applies to the adjusted gross income shown on your 1987 Form 1040, line 31, or Form 1040A, line 13. Your 1987 expenses must be within the 1987 limits.

Attach a computation showing how you figured the increase.
Line 8.—In certain cases, the amount of credit you figured on line 8 may be limited. Some taxpayers will need to complete **Form 6251,** Alternative Minimum Tax—Individuals, because the computation of this limit uses an amount from line 15 of that form. Other taxpayers, however, will not be affected by the limit and will not need Form 6251. The following will help you determine if you need Form 6251.
First, complete line 1 of the worksheet below.

Get Form 6251 if:
• You filed Schedule C, D, E, or F (Form 1040); OR
• The amount you enter on line 1 of the worksheet below is more than: $112,500 for single or head of household; $150,000 for married filing jointly; or $75,000 for married filing separately.

If **either** of the above applies to you, complete Form 6251 through line 15. Skip lines 2 through 6 of the worksheet and go directly to line A of the worksheet.
If **neither** of the above applies to you, continue with line 2 of the worksheet. You may still need to get Form 6251.

1. Enter the amount from Form 1040, line 23 . . . . _____
   (Add to line 1 any tax-exempt interest from private activity bonds issued after August 7, 1986, and any net operating loss deduction.)
2. Enter: $30,000 if single or head of household; $40,000 if married filing jointly; or $20,000 if married filing separately . . _____
3. Subtract line 2 from line 1. If the result is zero or less, **STOP HERE** and enter on Form 1040, line 41, the amount of your credit shown on line 8 of Form 2441. Otherwise, go on to line 4 . _____
4. Enter the amount from Form 1040, line 40 . . . . . _____
5. Multiply line 3 by .21 . . . _____
6. Subtract line 5 from line 4 (if zero or less, enter zero) . . . _____

Compare line 6 of the worksheet with the amount of credit shown on Form 2441, line 8.
• If line 6 (above) is more than your credit, you do not have to complete Form 6251. Enter on Form 1040, line 41, the amount of your credit shown on Form 2441, line 8.
• If your credit is more than the amount on line 6 (above), get Form 6251 and complete it through line 15. Then figure the limit on your credit as follows:
A. Enter amount from Form 1040, line 40 . . . . . . _____
B. Enter the amount from Form 6251, line 15 . . . . _____
C. **Maximum credit.** Subtract line B from line A (if zero or less, enter zero) . . . . _____

Compare the credit you first figured on line 8 of Form 2441 with line C above. Enter the **smaller** of the two amounts on line 8 of Form 2441, and on Form 1040, line 41. If line C above is the smaller amount, also write "AMT" in the left margin next to line 41.

☆U.S.GPO:1988-0-205-252

Appendices

Useful Lists of Resources

Homemade Recipes

PLAY DOUGH
> Mix: 1   cup flour
> 1/2 cup salt
> 1   Tbsp. oil
> 3   Tbsp. cream of tartar
> a couple of drops of food coloring
> 1   cup water

Heat and stir until it can't be stirred and forms a ball. It will still feel sticky. Cool and knead. Store in covered container.

ANOTHER PLAY DOUGH
> Mix: 1   cup flour
> 1/2 cup salt
> 1/4 cup water
> 1/4 cup oil
> food coloring

SMOOTH PLAY DOUGH
Mix: 2   cups of flour
        1/2   cup salt
        2   Tbsp. Alum
        2   Tbsp. oil
              food coloring

Boil 2 cups of water, add it into the mixture and stir (more flour if sticky)

PEANUT BUTTER PLAY DOUGH
Mix: 2   cups peanut butter
        1/2   cup powdered milk
        1/2   cup honey

Add powdered milk if the dough is too sticky.

CLOUD DOUGH
(like play dough but more elastic)
Mix: 1   cup salad oil
        6   cups flour
        1   cup water
              food coloring

OATMEAL PLAY DOUGH
Mix: 1   cup flour
        2   cups oatmeal
        1   cup water
              food color
              Add water gradually and mix

FACE PAINT
 Mix: 1   tsp. cornstarch
        1/2 tsp. water
        1/2 tsp. cold cream
             food coloring

 Combine cornstarch and water in small dish. Mix until smooth. Stir in food coloring and cold cream. Apply!

BAKED DOUGH
 Mix: 4   cups flour
        1   cup salt
        1 1/2 to 2 cups water
             condensed milk (brush on)
 Bake 250 degrees for one hour.
 Children use to make models that they can save.

MODELING GOOP
 Mix: 2   cups salt
        2/3 cup water
 Cook over medium heat for 5 minutes. Remove from heat.
 Mix: 1   cup corn starch
        1/2 cup water
 Add to salt mixture. Stir until smooth.
 Return mixture to low heat and stir until thick.

BUBBLES
Stir together: 3/4 cup liquid soap
                1/4 cup glycerine
                2   quarts water (8 cups)

GLITTER PAINT

Mix equal parts of flour, salt and water, add coloring. The salt glistens when dry. This works well as finger paint or from a squeeze bottle onto paper.

CRAFT CLAY

Mix:　　1　　cup cornstarch,
　　　　　2　　cups baking soda
　　　1 1/4　　cup water

Cook mixture until it thickens to dough-like consistency. Knead. Save in plastic bag. This clay works well for plaques or models and can be painted when it dries.

SOAP CRAYONS

Mix soap flakes with water and food coloring. Shape into crayons and let harden.

SILLY PUTTY

Mix together equal parts of Elmer's School Glue and liquid starch. Slowly add liquid starch to glue and knead with fingers. The more you work with it the better it gels. Add food coloring if you want.

Free Materials

Where to find them, how to use them

Materials	where to look for them	how to use them
paper	businesses,print shops, newspapers	art
wall paper	Paint and wallpaper stores	art
material scraps	interior design shops and fabric stores	art
telephone spools and poles	public service/phone company	large motor
large cardboard appliance boxes	appliance stores, dept. stores	play
old mattress	from parents	jumping/reading
carpet squares	carpet companies	group time
carpet remnants	carpet companies	floor covering
linoleum scraps	flooring company	art/carpentry
scrap lumber	lumber company, hardware store	carpentry/art
bricks, masonry	brick yards, demolished buildings	construction/blocks
ceramic tiles	hardware store, tile company	art/games
buttons	sewing stores	counting/sorting
tires, inner tubes	tire companies, garages	swings/bouncers
magazines, cards	card shop, stationery stores	collage/art
garden materials	gardening centers, nurseries	gardens/science
nuts and bolts	hardware store	small motor
egg cartons (paper)	from parents	art/construction
towel rolls, toilet	from parents	art/construction
paper rolls, milk	from parents	art/construction
cartons, L'eggs	from parents	art/construction
eggs, juice jars	from parents	art/construction
lids and jars, squeeze bottles	from parents	art/construction

Children's Magazine List

3-2-1 CONTACT

Published ten times a year by the Children's Television Workshop. Send subscription orders to 3-2-1 Contact, P.O. Box 53051, Boulder, CO, 80322-3051. Cost is $15.97 for one year. Articles and stories about nature, science, and technology designed for ages 8 to 14. Each issue is packed with puzzles, projects, and challenging square one TV math pages.

SCIENCELAND

Published eight times a year by Scienceland, Inc., 501 Fifth Avenue, New York, NY 10017-6165. Cost is $28.00 per year. Usually centered around one scientific topic with great pictures; for all ages.

STONE SOUP

Published five times a year (September, November, January, March, and May) by the Children's Art Foundation, P.O. Bo 83, Santa Cruz, CA 95063. Cost is $20.00 per year. Stories, poems, book reviews, and art by children through age 13. They encourage readers to send in their work.

RANGER RICK

Published monthly by the National Wildlife Federation, 8925 Leesburg Pike, Vienna, VA 22187-0001. Cost is $14.00 annually. Purpose is to help children age 6 to 12 learn more about the world of nature and conserving resources.

SESAME STREET

Published ten times a year by the Children's Television Workshop. Subscriber copies include two sections: Sesame Street Magazine and Parents' Guide. Send subscription orders to Sesame Street Magazine, P.O. Box 55518, Boulder, CO 80322-5518. Cost is $13.97 per year. Designed for children 2 through 6. Typically built around one theme per issue, the magazine reinforces concepts and ideas shown on the television program. Focuses on language arts, auditory and visual perception, self expression, and mathematical and reading skills. Available in Spanish and English.

OWL

Published ten times a year by The Young Naturalist Foundation, a nonprofit organization, with the aim of interesting children in their environment and the world around them. OWL is recommended for children over eight. Send subscription orders to Owl, P.O. Box 11314, Des Moines, IA 50340. Cost is $14.95 per year.

ODYSSEY

Published monthly by AstroMedia, 1027 N. 7th Street, Milwaukee, WI 53233. Cost is $21.00 per year. Space exploration and astronomy magazine for young people 8 to 14.

NATIONAL GEOGRAPHIC WORLD

Published monthly by the National Geographic Society, Department 00489, 17th and M Streets, NW, Washington, DC 20036. Cost is $10.95 annually. Children's version of the famed magazine.

JUNIOR SCHOLASTIC

Published biweekly during the school year by Scholastic, Inc., 730 Broadway, New York, NY 10003-9538. Cost is $5.25 per year. Centers on one basic topic with strong participation of the reader through a teacher's guide.

JACK AND JILL

Published monthly (except bimonthly February/March, April/May, June/July, and August/September) by Children's Better Health Institute, Benjamin Franklin Literary and Medical Society, Inc., at 1100 Waterway Boulevard, P.O. Box 567,. Indianapolis, IN 46206. Cost is $11.95 for one year. Health oriented magazine for children ages six to eight.

HUMPTY DUMPTY'S

Published monthly except bimonthly February/March, April/May, June/July, and August/September by Children's Better Health Institute, Benjamin Franklin Literary and Medical Society, Inc. at 1100 Waterway Boulevard, P.O. Box 567, Indianapolis, IN 46206. Cost is $11.95 for one year. Health oriented magazine for children ages four to six.

HIGHLIGHTS for Children

Published monthly (bimonthly July/August). Single issues are $2.95. Subscriptions should be sent to Highlights for Children, 2300 W. Fifth Avenue, P.O. Box 269, Columbus, OH 43272-0002. Goals include dedication to helping children grow in basic skills and knowledge, creativity, ability to think and reason, sensitivity to others, high ideals, and worthy ways of living.

KID CITY

Published monthly, except for February and August, by the Children's Television Workshop. Send subscriptions to Kid City, 200 Watt Street, P.O. Box 53349, Boulder, CO 80322. Cost is $13.97 per year. Designed for children ages six to ten. Makes reading, language skills and learning fun. Educates and entertains through stories, puzzles, word games, projects, and features. Perfect for Sesame Street graduates.

CRICKET

Published monthly by Carus Corporation, 315 Fifth Street, Peru, Il 61354. Cost is $24.97 per year. Literature magazine for children; perfect for bedtime stories or for older children to read to themselves.

COBBLESTONE

The history magazine for young people is published monthly by Cobblestone Publishing, Inc., 20 Grove Street, Petersborough, NH 03458. Cost is $19.95 annually. Usually centered on one theme in each issue. Teacher's guide also available. Strong participation and activity encouraged in each issue.

CHILDREN'S DIGEST

Published monthly (except bimonthly February/March, April/ May, June/July and August/September) by Children's Better Health Institute, Benjamin Franklin Literary & Medical Society, Inc. at 1100 Waterway Boulevard, P.O. Box 567, Indianapolis, IN 46206. Cost is $11.95 per year. Health oriented magazine for ages eight to ten. Activities and literature with lots of questions regarding health.

CHILD LIFE

Published monthly, except bimonthly February/March, April/ May, June/July and August/September by Children's Better Health Institute, Benjamin Franklin Literary & Medical Society, Inc. at 1100 Waterway Blvd., P.O. Box 567, Indianapolis, IN 46206. Cost is $11.95 per year. Health oriented magazine for ages seven to nine. Activities and literature with lots of questions regarding health.

BOYS' LIFE

Published monthly by the Boy Scouts of America, 1325 Walnut Hill Lane, P.O. Box 152079, Irving, TX 75015-2079. Cost is $13.20 a year. Designed for boys age 6 to 14. Stories and activities about other Boy Scouts.

CREATIVE KIDS

Published eight times a year by GCT Inc., 350 Weinacke Avenue, Mobile, AL 36604. Cost is $20.00 a year. Includes young people's work that represents their ideas, questions, fears, concerns and pleasures. Children are encouraged to submit their work for publication.

CHICKADEE

Published ten times a year by The Young Naturalist Foundation, a nonprofit organization, with the aim of interesting children in their environment and the world around them. Chickadee is recommended for children up to nine. Send subscription orders to Chickadee, P.O. Box 11314, Des Moines, IA 50340. Cost is $14.95 annually.

YOUR BIG BACKYARD
Published monthly by the National Wildlife Federation, 8925 Leesburg Pike, Vienna, VA 22184-0001. Cost is $14.00 annually. Purpose is to help children age three to five learn more about the world of nature and conserving resources. Letter to parents in each issue with suggestions on how to use pictures, games and puzzles in a creative way.

FACES
The magazine about people from around the world. Published monthly except July and August by Cobblestone Publishing, Inc., 20 Grove Street, Peterborough, NH 03458. Ten issues for $18.95.

Children's Book List

Allen, Pamela. *Who Sank the Boat?*. New York: Coward-McCann, 1983.

Anno, Mitsumasa. *Anno's Alphabet*. New York: Crowell Publications, 1975.

Anno, Mitsumasa. *Anno's Counting House*. New York: Philomel Books, 1982.

Anno, Mitsumasa. *Anno's U.S.A.* New York: Philomel Books, 1983.

Bailey, Carolyn Sherwin. *The Little Rabbit Who Wanted Red Wings*. New York: Platt and Munk Inc., 1961.

Barton, Alan. *Building a House*. New York: Greenwillow Books, 1981.

Battles, Edith. *What Does The Rooster Say, Yoshio?* Chicago: Whitman Press, 1978.

Bemelmans, Ludwig I. *Madeline*. New York: Viking Press, 1960.

Blaine, Marge. *The Terrible Thing That Happened at Our House*. New York: Parent's Magazine Press, 1975.

Bright, Robert. *Georgie*. Garden City: Doubleday Press, 1944.

Bright, Robert. *Georgie and the Robbers*. Garden City: Doubleday Press, 1963.

Burton, Virginia Lee. *Katy and the Big Snow*. Boston: Houghton Mifflin, 1943.

Burton, Virginia Lee. *Mike Mulligan and His Steam Shovel*. Boston: Houghton Mifflin, 1930.

Carle, Eric. *The Very Hungry Caterpillar*. New York: World Books, 1969.

Carle, Eric. *The Very Busy Spider*. New York: Philomel Books, 1985.

Carle, Eric. *The Mixed-Up Chameleon*. New York: Philomel Books, 1984.

Carle, Eric. *The Grouchy Ladybug*. New York: Crowell Co., 1977.

Charao, Kay. *Kate's Quilt*. New York: EP Dutton, 1982.

Charao, Kay. *Kate's Car*. New York: EP Dutton, 1982.

Charao, Kay. *Lester's Overnight*. New York: EP Dutton, 1977.

Clifton, Lucille. *The Boy Who Didn't Believe in Spring*. New York: EP Dutton, 1973.

Cohen, Miriam. *Will I Have a Friend?* New York: Macmillan, 1967.

Crews, Donald. *Freight Train.* New York: Greenwillow Books, 1978.

Crews, Donald. *Carousel.* New York: Greenwillow Books, 1982.

Crews, Donald. *Truck.* New York: Greenwillow Books, 1980.

Crowe, Robert L. *Clyde Monster.* New York: EP Dutton, 1976.

DeBrunhoff, Jean. *Babar and His Children.* New York: Random House, 1966.

Delage, Ida. *Am I a Bunny?.* Champaign: Garrard Publishing Co., 1978.

DePaola, Tomi. *Oliver Button is a Sissy.* New York: Harcourt Brace Jovanovich Publishing, 1979.

DeRegniers, Beatrice. *May I Bring A Friend?* New York: Atheneum, 1964.

Dr. Seuss. *Horton Hatches the Egg.* New York: Random House, 1940.

Dr. Seuss. *Green Eggs and Ham.* New York: Beginner Books, 1960.

Dr. Seuss. *One Fish, Two Fish, Red Fish, Blue Fish.* New York: Beginner Books, 1957.

Dr. Seuss. *Hop On Pop.* New York: Beginner Books, 1963.

Dr. Seuss. *Cat in the Hat Comes Back.* New York: Beginner Books, 1958.

Flack, Marjorie. *Ask Mr. Bear.* New York: Macmillan, 1932.

Freeman, Don. *Norman the Doorman.* New York: Viking Press, 1959.

Freeman, Don. *Pocket for Corduroy.* New York: Viking Press, 1978.

Gag, Wanda. *Millions of Cats.* New York: Coward-McCann, 1928.

Goodall, John S. *Naughty Nancy Goes to School.* New York: Atheneum, 1985.

Goodall, John S. *An Edwardian Summer.* New York: Atheneum, 1976.

Goodall, John S. *An Edwardian Christmas.* New York: Atheneum, 1978.

Gramtky, Hardie. *Little Toot.* New York: Putnam, 1939.

Greenberg, Hardie. *The Bravest Babysitter.* New York: Dial Press, 1977.

Haas, Irene. *The Maggie B.* New York: Atheneum, 1975.

Barthelme, Donald. *Snow White.* New York: Atheneum, 1967.

Heller, Ruth. How to Hide a Polar Bear. New York: Grosset and Dunlap, 1986.

Heller, Ruth. *How to Hide a Butterfly*. New York: Grosset and Dun--lap, 1985.

Hill, Eric. *Where's Spot*. New York: Putnam, 1987.

Hill, Eric. *Spot's Birthday Party*. New York: Putnam, 1982.

Hill, Eric. *Spot's First Christmas*. New York: Putnam, 1983.

Hill, Eric. *Spot's First Walk*. New York: Putnam, 1981.

Hoban, Tana. *Is It Larger? Is It Smaller?*. New York: Greenwillow Books, 1985.

Hoff, Syd. *When Will It Snow?*. New York: Harper and Row, 1971.

Hughes, Shirley. *Alfie Gives a Hand*. New York: Lothrop, Lee, and Shepard Books, 1983.

Hutchins, Pat. *Titch*. New York: Macmillan Books, 1971.

Hutchins, Pat. *Rosie's Walk*. New York: Macmillan Books, 1967.

Kellogg, Steven. *Can I Keep Him?*. New York: Dial Press, 1971.

Johnson, Crockett I. *Harold and the Purple Crayon*. New York: Harper, 1955.

Johnson, Tony. *The Quilt Story*. New York: Putnam, 1985.

Keats, Ezra Jack. *Peter's Chair*. New York: Harper and Row, 1967.

Keats, Ezra Jack. *The Snowy Day*. New York: Viking Press, 1962.

Keats, Ezra Jack. *Dreams*. New York: Macmillan, 1974.

Keats, Ezra Jack. *Whistle for Willie*. New York: Viking Press, 1964.

Keats, Ezra Jack. *Over in the Meadow*. New York: Four Winds Press, 1971.

Kraus, Robert. *Leo the Late Bloomer*. New York: Windmill Books, 1971.

Kraus, Robert. *Milton the Early Riser*. New York: Windmill Books, 1972.

Kraus, Robert. *Owliver*. New York: Windmill Books, 1974.

Kraus, Robert. *Whose Mouse Are You?*. New York: Macmillan, 1969.

Krauss, Ruth. *The Carrot Seed*. New York: Harper, 1945.

Langstaff, Leo. *Frog Went A Courtin'*. New York: Harcourt, Brace, 1955.

Leaf, Munro. *The Story of Ferdinand*. New York: Viking Press, 1936.

Lionni, Leo. *Swimmy*. New York: Pantheon, 1968.

Lionni, Leo. The Biggest House in the World. New York: Pantheon, 1968.

Lionni, Leo. *Frederick*. New York: Pantheon, 1967.

Lionni, Leo. *Aleander and the Wind-up Mouse*. New York: Pantheon, 1967.

Lionni, Leo. *Fish is Fish*. New York: Pantheon, 1970.

Lionni, Leo. *A Color of His Own*. New York: Pantheon, 1975.

Lionni, Leo. *Little Blue and Little Yellow*. New York: McDowell, Obolensky, 1959.

McCloskey, Robert. *Make Way for Ducklings*. New York: Viking Press, 1941.

McCloskey, Robert. *Blueberries for Sal*. New York: Viking Press, 1948.

McCloskey, Robert. *Lentil*. New York: Viking Press, 1940.

McDermott, Gerald. *Arrow to the Sun*. New York: Viking Press, 1974.

McDermott, Gerald. *Anansi*. New York: Holt, Reinhart, and Winston, 1974.

McDermott, Gerald. *The Magic Tree*. New York: Holt, Reinhart, and Winston, 1973.

McKee, David. *I Hate My Teddy Bear*. New York: Clarion Books, 1984.

McPhail, David M. *The Bear's Toothache*. Boston: Little Brown, 1972.

McPhail, David M. *Pig Pig Grows Up*. New York: Dutton Books, 1980.

Marshall, James. *George and Martha One Fine Day*. Boston: Houghton Mifflin, 1978.

Marshall, James. *Professor Wormbog in Search of Zippernup*. New York: Golden Press, 1976.

Mayer, Mercer. *Liza Lou and the Yeller Belly Swamp*. New York: Parent's Magazine Press, 1976.

Mayer, Mercer. *East of the Sun, West of the Moon*. New York: Four Winds Press, 1980.

Mayer, Mercer. *There's a Nightmare in My Closet*. New York: Dial Press, 1968.

Mayer, Mercer. *Just For You.* New York: Golden Press, 1975.

Mayer, Mercer. *Just Me and My Dad.* New York: Golden Press, 1977.

Mayer, Mercer. *Brown Bear, Brown Bear, What do You See?.* New York: Holt, Reinhart, and Winston, 1983.

Ness, Evaline. *Sam, Bangs, and Moonshine.* New York: Holt, Reinhart, and Winston, 1966.

Nekatani, Chiyoko. *My Teddy Bear.* New York: Crowell, 1976.

Numeroff, Laura Joffe. *If You Give a Mouse a Cookie.* New York: Harper and Row, 1985.

Piper, Watty. *The Little Engine that Could.* New York: Platt and Munk Co., 1930.

Potter, Beatrix. *Peter Rabbit-Giant Treasury.* New York: Derrydale Books, 1980.

Potter, Beatrix. *The Tale of the Flopsy Bunnies.* New York: Warne, 1909.

Rey, Margret Elisabeth Waldstein. *Curious George.* Boston: Houghton Mifflin, 1941.

Rey, Margret Elisabeth Waldstein. *Curious George goes to the Hospital.* Boston: Houghton Mifflin, 1966.

Rockwell, Anne F. *Cars.* New York: Dutton, 1984.

Rockwell, Anne F. *Trucks.* New York: Dutton, 1984.

Rockwell, Anne F. *Boats.* New York: Dutton, 1982.

Scheer, Julian. *Rain Makes Applesauce.* New York: Holiday House, 1964.

Sendak, Maurice. *Outside Over There.* New York: Harper and Row, 1981.

Sendak, Maurice. *Where The Wild Things Are.* New York: Caedmon, 1988.

Sendak, Maurice. *In the Night Kitchen.* New York: Harper and Row, 1970.

Sendak, Maurice. *One Was Johnny.* New York: Harper and Row, 1962.

Sendak, Maurice. *Chicken Soup with Rice.* New York: Harper and Row, 1962.

Shaw, Charles Green. *It Looked Like Spilt Milk.* New York: Harper and Row, 1947.

Silverstein, Shel. *The Light in the Attic*. New York: Harper and Row, 1981.

Silverstein, Shel. *The Giving Tree*. New York: Harper and Row, 1964.

Silverstein, Shel. *The Missing Piece*. New York: Harper and Row, 1976.

Spier, Peter. *Rain*. New York: Doubleday, 1982.

Spier, Peter. *People*. New York: Doubleday, 1980.

Spier, Peter. *Gobble, Growl, Grunt*. New York: Doubleday, 1971.

Spier, Peter. *Gilberto and the Wind*. New York: Viking Press, 1963.

Steig, William. *Sylvester and the Magic Pebble*. New York: Windmill Books, 1969.

Stevenson, Robert Louis. *A Child's Garden of Verses*. New York: Watts, 1966.

Tafuri, Nancy. *All Year Long*. New York: Greenwillow Books, 1983.

Tafuri, Nancy. *Have You Seen My Duckling?*. New York: Greenwillow Books, 1984.

Testa, Fulvio. *If You Seek Adventure*. New York: Dial Books for Young Readers, 1984.

Viorst, Judith. *Aleander, Who Used To Be Rich Last Sunday*. New York: Atheneum, 1977.

Viorst, Judith. *Aleander and the Terrible, Horrible, No Good, Very Bad Day*. New York: Atheneum, 1972.

Viorst, Judith. *My Mama Says There Aren't Any Zombies....* New York: Atheneum, 1973.

Watanabe, Shigeo. *Where's My Daddy?*. New York: Philomel Books, 1982.

Watanabe, Shigeo. *How Do I Put It On?* New York: Collins, 1979.

Watanabe, Shigeo. *I'm the King of the Castle*. New York: Philomel Books, 1982.

Watanabe, Shigeo. *What a Good Lunch*. New York: Collings Publications, 1928.

Wise, Margret Brown. *The Important Book*. New York: Harper and Row, 1949.

Wise, Margret Brown. *The Friendly Book*. Racine: Golden Press, 1975.

Wood, Audrey. *Quick as a Cricket*. New York: Child's Play International Ltd., 1982.

Yashima, Taro. *Crow Boy*. New York: Viking Press, 1955.
Yashima, Taro. *Umbrella*. New York: Viking Press, 1958.
Zemach, Margot. *It Could Always Be Worse*. New York: Farrar, Straus, Girou, 1976.
Zion, Gene. *Harry the Dirty Dog*. New York: Harper and Row, 1956.
Zion, Gene. *No Roses for Harry*. New York: Harper and Row, 1958.
Zolotow, Charlotte. *The Hating Book*. New York: Harper and Row, 1969.
Zolotow, Charlotte. *William's Doll*. New York: Harper and Row, 1972.

Bibliography

Books

Black, Helen R.D. *The Great Co-op Food Book*. Berkeley: Bull Publishing Company, December, 1979.

Blank, Helen. *Child Care: The Time Is Now*. Washington: Children's Defense Fund, 1986.

Bredekamp, Sue (Editor). *Accreditation Criteria and Procedures of the National Academy of Early Childhood Programs and Possibilities*. Washington: National Association for the Education of Young Children, 1984.

"Child Care Information Exchange." *The Director's Magazine*. Redmond: Craftsman Press, Bimonthly issues, 1989.

Children's Defense Fund. "The Child Care Handbook: Needs, Programs, and Possibilities." Washington: 1982.

Colorado State University Cooperative Extension Office. "Good Times With Child Care." Fort Collins: Extension Service Bulletin Room, Bulletin #544A, 1989.

Division of the Bureau of National Affairs. Washington: The National Report on Work and Family, 1988.

Education Commission of the States. "Choices For Children: Policy Options for State Provision of Early Childhood Programs." Denver: 1988.

Friedman, Dana E. "Special Report: Child Care for Employee's Kids." Harvard Business Review, 1986.

Friesen, Anne. "Mile High Child Care Honors Denver's Pioneers in Child Care." Denver: Mile High Child Care, 1988.

Frost, Joe L. and Wortham, Sue C. "The Evolution of American Playgrounds." *Young Children*. Denver: National Association for the Education of Young Children, July, 1988.

Galinsky, Ellen., Hughes, Diane. "The Fortune Magazine Child Care Study." Bank Street College commissioned by *Fortune Magazine*, December, 1986.

Gnezda, Therese M., Shelley L. Smith. "Child Care and Early Childhood Education Policy: A Legislator's Guide." National Conference of State Legislators, March, 1989.

Hewes, Dorothy, "NAEYC's First Half Century 1926-1970." NAEYC Organizational History and Archives Committee, *Young Children*, September, 1976.

Highlights Creative Craft Series. ("128 Holiday Crafts Kids Can Make," "Party Ideas With Crafts Kids Can Make," "127 Anytime Crafts Kids Can Make," "132 Gift Crafts Kids Can Make.") Columbus: Highlights for Children, Inc., 1981.

Ingassia, Lawrence. "Day Care Business Lures Entrenpreneurs." Wall Street Journal, June 3, 1988. Dow Jones and Co. Inc.

Johnston, William B. "Work Force 2000, Work and Workers for the 21st Century, Executive Summary." Hudson Institute, June, 1987.

Kaplan, . "How To Open Your Own Child Care Center." New York: Supplement to *Scholastic Pre-K Today*. May/June, 1989.

Moore, Amy J. "Child Care for Rosie the Riveter's Kids." Child Care Action News, July/August, 1988.

Morgan, Gwen. *The National State of Child Care Regulation 1986*. Watertown: Work/Family Directions Inc., 1987.

NASBE Task Force on Early Childhood Education. "Right from the Start." Alexandria: National Association of State Boards of Education, 1988.

National Association for the Education of Young Children. "Young Children." Washington: NAEYC Journal, Bimonthly issue, 1989.

Sher, Margey Leveen, Gary Braun. "What To Do With Jenny—A Corporate Child Decision that Greatly Affects the Bottom Line." Personnel Administrator, April, 1989.

Resources for Child Caring. St. Paul: Toys 'n Things Press, A Division of Resources for Child Caring, Inc., 1989.

Other References

Arnold, Arnold. *The World Book Of Children's Games*. Greenwich: Fawcett-Crest, 1973.

Bannet-Stein, Sarah. *The Kids Kitchen Take-Over*. New York: Workman Publishing, 1975.

Beckman, Carol with Roberta Simmons, Nancy Thomas. *Channels to Children*. Colorado Springs: Channels to Children, 1982.

Beers-Boguslawski, Dorothy. *Guide for Establishing and Operating Day Care Centers for Young Children*. New York: Child Welfare League of America, 1986.

Blank, H. and Wilkins, A. *State Child Care Factbook*. Washington: Children's Defense Fund, 1987.

Bredekamp, Sue. *Developmentally Appropriate Practices*. Washington: National Association for the Education of Young Children, 1988.

Cole, Ann, with Carolyn Haas, Elizabeth Heller, Betty Weinberger. *A Pumpkin In A Pear Tree*. Boston: Little, Brown, and Company, 1976.

Comfort, Randy Lee, Constance D. Williams. *The Child Care Catalog*. Littleton: Libraries Unlimited, Inc., 1985.

Derman-Sparks, Louse and ABC Task Force. Anti-Bias Curriculum, *Tools for Empowering Young Children*. Washington: National Association for the Education of Young Children, 1988-89.

Dondiego, Barbara. *Crafts For Kids, A Month By Month Idea Book*. Blue Ridge Summit: TAB Books Inc., 1984.

Dublin-Keyserling, Mary. *Windows on Day Care*. "A Report Based on Findings of the National Council of Jewish Women".

Forte, Imogene. *The Table Top Learning Series*. ("Science Fun," "Games", "Arts And Crafts," others.) Nashville: Incentive Publications Inc., 1983-1985.

Goffin, Stacie G. and Lombardi, Joan. *Speaking Out: Early Childhood Advocacy*. Washington: National Association for the Education of Young Children, 1989.

Gregson, Bob. *The Incredible Indoor Games Book*. Belmont: David S.Lake Publishers, 1982.

Grubb, W. Norton. "America's Child Care Needs." Washington: American Federation of State, County, and Municipal Employees (AFSCME), 1987.

Hepworth-Berger, Eugenia, Ph.D. *Parents As Partners In Education*. St. Louis: C.V. Mosby Company, 1981.

Holmman, Mary, Bernard Banet, and David Weikart. *Young Children In Action*. Ypsilanti: High/Scope Press, 1979.

Indenbaum, Valerie. *The Everything Book for Teachers of Young Children*. Lavonia: Partner Press, 1985.

Jorde-Bloom, Paula. *A Great Place To Work*. Washington: National Association for the Education of Young Children, 1988-89.

Lansky, Vicki. *Feed Me I'm Yours*. Wazata: Meadowbrook Press, 1977.

Marzollo, Jean, with Janice Lloyd. *Learning Through Play*. New York:, 1972.

Miller, Karen. *Ages And Stages*. Marshfield: TelShare Publishing Co., 1985.

Things To Do With Toddlers And Twos. Marshfield: TelShare Publishing Co., 1984.

Moore, Nancy. *Who Sez There's Nothing To Do?* Aurora: Moore and Allen Partnership, 1989.

Morgan, G. *The National State of Child Care Regulation 1986*. Watertown: Work/Family Directions Inc., 1987.

Morris, Nancy L. *Simple Projects For Young Children From Nancy's House*. Denver: Wildwood Resources Inc., 1986.

Phillips, D.A. *Quality in Child Care: What Does Research Tell Us?* Washington: National Association for the Education of Young Children, 1987.

Veitch, Beverly and Harms, Thelma. *Cook and Learn*: Mealo Park, California. 1981.

Wolfgang, Charles H., Bea Mackender, Mary E. Wolfgang. *Growing and Learning Through Play*. New York: McGraw Hill Publishing, 1981.

Willer, B. *The Growing Crisis in Child Care: Quality, Compensation, and Affordability in Early Childhood Programs*. Washington: National Association for the Education of Young Children, 1987.

Index

Forms Kit For Directors

This easy-to-use, comprehensive forms package provides 30 reproducible forms to cover your every need. Covering "Health and
Safety", "Registration/Intake", "Observations", "Evaluations", and
other topic areas. You'll save time and effort with these field-tested
forms.

Please send me_____ forms kits.

☐ Check or money order enclosed

* Charge my ☐ Visa ☐ Mastercard

Account #_____ Expiration Date_____

Signature _____

Name _____ Phone (_____)_____

Address_____

City/State/Zip _____

Enclose $7.95 each, plus $2.00 postage and handling per book.
(Colorado residents please add $1.05 state sales tax.)
Canadian orders must be accompanied by a *postal money order in
U.S. Funds.*
Allow 30 days for delivery.

Make checks payable to:VMP Inc.
     6900 West Alameda Avenue #301
     Lakewood, CO 80226
     Call (303) 935-6703 for credit card orders

Quantity Orders Invited
For quantity discount prices or special UPS handling, call
(303) 935-6703.

Did You Borrow This Book?

Want A Copy For A Friend Or Colleague?

YES, I want to invest $14.95 in my future. Please send_____ copies of **The Everyday Guide to Opening and Operating a Child Care Center.**

☐ Check or money order enclosed

* Charge my ☐ Visa ☐ Mastercard

Account # _____ Expiration Date_____

Signature _____

Name _____ Phone (____)_____

Address_____

City/State/Zip _____

Enclose $14.95 each, plus $2.00 postage and handling per book. (Colorado residents please add $1.05 state sales tax.) Canadian orders must be accompanied by a *postal money order in U.S. Funds.* Allow 30 days for delivery.

Make checks payable to: VMP Inc.
       6900 West Alameda Avenue #301
       Lakewood, CO 80226
       Call (303) 935-6703 for credit card orders

Quantity Orders Invited
For quantity discount prices or special UPS handling, call (303) 935-6703.